M000224287

THE
SPAMALOT
DIARIES

———

ALSO BY ERIC IDLE

"Hello Sailor"
(Weidenfeld & Nicolson/Futura, 1975)

The Rutland Dirty Weekend Book
(Eyre Methuen, 1976)

Pass the Butler: A Play
(Methuen, 1984)

*The Quite Remarkable Adventures of
the Owl and the Pussycat*
(Dove Books, 1996)

The Road to Mars: A Postmodern Novel
(Pantheon, 1999)

The Greedy Bastard Diary: A Comic Tour of America
(Harper Entertainment, 2005)

The Writer's Cut: A Hollywood Novel
(Canelo ebook, 2015)

Always Look on the Bright Side of Life: A Sortabiography
(Crown Archetype, 2018)

In loving memory of Mike Nichols,
the greatest and the best

CONTENTS

THE
SPAMALOT
DIARIES

———

INTRODUCTION

I was friends with Mike Nichols for fifteen years before Bill Haber asked me who I wanted to direct *Spamalot*. Bill had come to tea with Tania and me at our home in the Hollywood Hills. He had just bought the play for Broadway in twenty minutes after I gave him a script and played him a couple of songs, and he was on his way out the front gate when he asked that vital question.

Without a second's hesitation I replied, "Oh, Mike."

"Mike Nichols?"

"Absolutely. He's a pal. I've known him fifteen years."

"Well, he's a friend of mine, too," said Bill, "but he takes ages to respond."

"So send him the script and the demo of the songs; he *really* likes our songs."

"Well, I will," said Bill, "but don't hold your breath."

Three days later the phone rang. It was Mike.

"Yes, yes, yes" was all he said.

In all those fifteen years of friendship, in many far-flung places around the world, Mike and I never argued or disagreed or had any kind of falling-out. It was always laughter, theater, dinner, and comedy. Once in Saint-Paul de Vence, passing an art gallery with me, Mike spotted a skinny sculpture on display behind the glass. He popped his head in and said, "How much is that Dalí in the window?"

It reduced me to hysterics.

Even when we were on vacation with him in Barbados our holiday snaps were by Avedon. Of course. They were best pals. Mike was first class all the way. So when we began working on *Spamalot* we were the best of chums, but working together is totally different from being on holiday, and as it happened we disagreed on many things. Of course. Disputes over details are an important part of the process and I have deliberately left these moments in, because they show that it is possible to disagree with someone and still continue happily working together. During the Monty Python writing sessions we would argue vociferously about everything, about every tiny detail, about what kind of a chair it should be, about what sort of bird should be dead, and especially about where we should go to film. Disagreement is healthy and normal. It's comedy. It's that serious!

I began writing *Spamalot* at the beginning of 2001. In the mid-nineties I had been working on a CD-ROM game of *Monty Python and the Holy Grail* for 7th Level. Having written and produced a musical for BBC Radio Four in the eighties, John Du Prez and I had been looking for a good subject for a stage musical when I suddenly realized it was right under our feet. Of course, the Holy Grail! I realized that if the Python film could spawn a game, it might also adapt into a musical. It already had three great songs, there are no horses onstage, and the quest for the Holy Grail itself is Wagnerian in scope. Not the Ring cycle exactly, more the Rinse cycle.

John and I had just returned from the Greedy Bastard Tour, a fifteen-thousand-mile, three-month comedy tour across North America in a rock and roll bus. I had blogged our progress daily from the road, and so now, leaving home again, I must have continued with my habit of jotting down my thoughts first thing in the morning. I had completely forgotten I'd kept this diary until last year, when we were moving from our old home in the Hollywood Hills to something smaller with no stairs. I call this process Downsize Abbey, and it's amazing the things that turn up. Just how much crap can two people accommodate? I went to boarding school, but it might as well have been hoarding school for the amount of rubbish we had collected. We had two lockups filled with everything from old Monty Python scripts to hundreds of Beanie Babies that one day, apparently, we were going to sell for a small fortune. Yeah, right. And who needs twenty-seven guitars? Me, apparently. I still only have two hands. Or four thousand books? I realized I didn't have time to read them again, so off they went to a bookshop in Covina. Let some other people read 'em.

Even weirder things turned up as we began to catalogue what was useful and what was just shite. One of the most unexpected was this *Spamalot* diary. A friend read it and said they enjoyed it, then my wife read it and cried, and then another friend said they'd loved it and, well, thank you, friends, this is all your fault. It tells the story of a most unlikely theatrical hit, from the first read-through in New York to the first previews in Chicago until, finally, a Broadway opening. It lays the blame for success squarely on Bill Haber; Mike Nichols; Casey Nicholaw; and of course my musical partner, John Du Prez. It was a roller coaster of a ride, and I am grateful to many people, but this book is dedicated to Mike Nichols. It was the best working relationship I have ever experienced as a writer. He was the kindest and the funniest and the most encouraging person I have ever met, and I loved him dearly. And of course to beloved Casey, the quiet genius.

It took a long time for all the various parties to agree and by the time this diary opens in the spring of 2004 Bill Haber has bought the rights, the Pythons have consented to take one third of the artistic royalties for the underlying rights (a new Broadway record; the norm is 25 percent), Mike Nichols is on board to direct, he has discovered the uniquely talented Casey Nicholaw for our choreographer, we are seven drafts and twenty songs in, and I am flying to New York for the first read of what we hope will be our Broadway cast when we begin scheduled rehearsals in the fall.

It was the best of times. . . .

Eric Idle
California
December 2023

PART I

—

To New York City for the First Read

TUESDAY, APRIL 20, 2004

Okay, now finally it's real!

It was rainy and cold when I landed, but soon the sun came out and the blossoms popped; and in the five days I have been here Central Park has turned from brown sticks to pointillist green outside my window at the Essex House hotel. I remember at the old Navarro Hotel, in the height of summer, watching them spraying the park's grass green, but this time it is purely Mother Nature, though perhaps Motherfucker Nature might be a more appropriate soubriquet for New York.

WEDNESDAY, APRIL 21, 2004

So to our big first meeting when we assemble in Shubert Alley off 44th and Broadway for our initial look at the Shubert Theatre, which will be our home next year. There are about a dozen people waiting outside when I arrive on the dot of ten, having limped down Broadway. Composer John Du Prez is there with Bill Haber, our producer, and Peter Lawrence, our stage manager. Wendy Orshan and Jeff Wilson, our producers from 101 Productions, introduce me to our choreographer, Casey Nicholaw; the set and costume designer, Tim Hatley; and our lighting designer, Hugh Vanstone. Mike Nichols arrives last and is hailed by all and we squeeze through the stage door and onto the stage. So this finally is it. We all wander around like excited schoolkids, chattering happily.

From the stage, the house seems much smaller than I had imagined. Seating only thirteen hundred it feels intimate compared to some that John Du Prez and I have played on our tours. Three slices, but even the high nosebleed balcony doesn't feel so far away. Nowhere is more than fifty-five feet from the stage. It also doesn't seem very deep, and we discuss how to get a police car on, which is our current ending. We all look knowledgeably up into the flies, which are, of course, the bits on the front of a pair of trousers. You'll see I am quickly learning all about the theater. For instance I notice immediately that Row C, Seat 101, is invisible from the balcony, so we will have to alter the song when the Knights discover the Grail under a seat in the audience and drag them up on stage to reward them. We will make it Row A, Seat 101.

After about an hour of this Mike and I repair to the offices of Mike's production company, Icarus, on the corner of 57th by Carnegie Hall. An interesting choice of name. Mike must feel he is constantly flying too close to the sun and that disaster will strike any moment. I tell him I have decided to call my company Lazarus. Back from the dead . . .

Casey has the brightest eyes and a great big beaming smile and he is very cuddly and warm. He reminds me we worked together before. His last performance was as one of the dancing crows in *Seussical*, a musical I wrote the treatment for, and we had met in Toronto. He is so happy Mike has chosen him for his first Broadway show as choreographer, which displays enormous faith by Mike, and he is full of ideas of what to do, including one fanfare farting chorus, which actually makes me laugh, though before we can pitch it, Mike warns we may only have two fart jokes in any one production. This must be some kind of Broadway rule of thumb. Perhaps from the days of Noël Coward.

"Gertrude, darling, that is your last fart joke."

"Oh, piss off, Noël, you silly billy."

THURSDAY, APRIL 22, 2004

As I was limping down Seventh Avenue yesterday, a passing rickshaw cyclist insisted he give me a ride. A mysterious tendon injury which had me hopping around on my tour is awaiting a final diagnosis and an operation. Being the philosopher I am and still quite lame, I hopped aboard. It was hilarious. I decided I must arrive for the premiere like this. Apart from the view, which is unfortunately mainly the cyclist's ass, it's a tremendous ride. Joe was a burly out-of-work actor, so I had to peer on either side of his wide rear end to see the various landmarks. As I passed down the street at pedestrian height, people kept recognizing me and doing double takes. Of course I pretended I was Michael Palin and that I was making a travel program. Around the Bronx in eighty days.

When I arrived at the theater, Peter Lawrence walked me in. I sat in his warren of an office and went through our stage directions with him for the reading. It really is a rabbit hole backstage, like being inside Nelson's flagship H.M.S. *Victory*. You have to bend double. Lots of head-banging potential and warning signs. I don't know how they are all going to cope. There are some sight-line issues at the Shubert, but the sound issues are horrendous. Last night I had gone to see Bernadette Peters perform here in *Gypsy*, and for the first ten minutes when she arrived onstage there were very loud sirens, followed by the deep, angry hooting of a blocked fire engine. They promise they are going to sound-proof the rear emergency doors, but it would need a whole set of second doors to achieve anything worthwhile. John and I immediately wrote a song about waiting for the Sirens to go, which our cast might launch into when appropriate.

I bump into Bill Haber outside the Shubert Theatre. He is always so jolly and so dapper and so funny. How could he ever have been an agent? We discuss putting something up outside on the wall in Shubert Alley. Currently there is a huge painted sign proclaiming *Gypsy*. I suggest a large Gilliam foot and the words *Run Away*. I feel there should be lots of flags for *Spamalot*.

Bill says the big issues so far are money, money, and money. The costs are rising precipitously. It was eight million dollars, then eleven, now I hear rumors of thirteen. I joked to someone the other day that our lawyers cost more than the original movie. True, by the way. The budget of the *Holy Grail* movie was only $400,000. Bill says it will take two years till we break even. It takes that long to recoup the costs. They even suggested we use just three chorus girls, instead of six. That's ridiculous. You cannot have only three maidens in Castle Anthrax.

Everyone blames the theater owners who, over the years, have given more to the unions, without taking less for rent, so that incoming producers have all these built-in costs they cannot control and they simply cannot make any money. Flying is expensive, too, and I suggest we cut the proposed witch escape, but Mike is adamant:

"No young women get burned in any production of mine," he says.

It's probably as well Mike hasn't tackled Shaw's *Saint Joan*.

Subj: Re: (no subject)
Date: 4/22/2004, 7:00 a.m., eastern daylight time
From: Eric Idle
To: Mike Nichols

Hello, mein Führer.

Is that too formal?

I was just checking in and hoping you were as excited as I was yesterday.

This is a big dream come true for me and I can only hope and pray it all ends in tears. That after all is the fate of Icarus.

I suppose the English equivalent would be flying too close to the rain.

I am going to stand at the back of the Shubert tonight and see how it all looks. I may even yell out *Ni*.

Eddie Izzard just offered his services Saturday morning for the read. He is flying in tonight. I think he may be too late but I told everyone who should know and they are on to it. He wanted to come by and watch. I told him it was deeply private. Not sure how you feel about that, but best to keep it in the family, right?

Subj: Re: (no subject)
Date: 4/22/2004, 6:00 p.m., eastern daylight time
From: Mike Nichols
To: Eric Idle

right. i don't think we should put our friends/readers in that position. we agree.

i am also excited. a little more tentatively since i am the one who mustn't fuck up.

it's not like your piece is untested and we will see if it is worthy. it is a little like taking on piloting the queen mary on her 10th voyage, with all speed records won already. no. it is like conducting beehoven's ninth in salzburg. no, conducting rosenkavalier in vienna. no,

more like repainting brueghel's "the fall of icarus." that's
not quite what i mean. it's like . . . oh forget it.

　i am excited and we will not rest till it is the best and
funniest musical ever performed. xoxxm

FRIDAY, APRIL 23, 2004

It is Shakespeare's birthday. He is four hundred and forty
today. I can't find a card with that age on it and I doubt Strat-
ford graveyard accepts mail anyway. Still, they do put out
flags and parade in the streets every year, so maybe he won't
notice.

We begin at nine in Mike's offices at Icarus, John and I
with Casey, a lovely and very funny man, going through the
dance numbers. There is discussion about lengthening most
of the dances, but I have this dream of a really tight and fast-
moving production, like *Oh! What a Lovely War*, where
nothing stays on for very long.

Mike has some brilliant ideas he shares, and a few concerns. He wants Patsy and Arthur to emerge riding, from
under the stage, which is a very nice idea. A large ramp is to
be built to accommodate this, which we could also use for
the arrival of the Killer Rabbit. Mike confesses to me he
doesn't like the Killer Rabbit, and I have to persuade him
that for our flimsy plot we really cannot omit it at this point.
However I do see a way to having only *one* knight decapi-
tated, and not the whole mass of them, when attacked by the

Vicious Killer Bunny of Caerbannagh. This will help us to get on with the play at this point. Mike also confesses to a dislike for the Knights of Ni, but when we act it out together, i.e., I say *Ni!* and he pretends to be scared, it gets us both laughing uncontrollably and he is now convinced that it works.

Some other great suggestions: the Black Knight is to be done in the manner of the Black Light Theatre of Prague, with black-robed people holding a limb each, giving the illusion of a knight who can be sliced apart. I make a note that even the head can be lopped off and carry on abusing Arthur. I like it because this way there need be no blood. Apart from being an audience turnoff, it is also slippery and dangerous onstage.

At noon we are joined by Tim Hatley and Hugh Vanstone and we go through the show, talking about sets and what happens onstage. Tim Hatley, who is soon dubbed "Tim the Enchanting," uses *fuck-off* freely as an adjective.

"We have these big fuck-off clumps of reeds."

Tim seems absolutely au courant with everything and it is wonderful he is also doing the costumes. His stage designs are spectacular and in parts downright inspired. He has an impressive practicality about him, a concern for how things are done; and Hugh also breathes quiet confidence. They seem to have done everything and frequently together. There is a recurring reference to British Pantomime, which reassures me, since that is largely what we are doing. They even talk about a whiffenpoof, which is some kind of feather boa on a string that is a great panto prop.

Mike loves the "Cow Song," but he wants the actor to sing it as a torch song and we discuss various ways to see her face. Tim and I favor some kind of opening up of the cow mask so it becomes like a Paris hat on a Dior cow. I suggest she should sit on the stage à la Judy Garland. Mike also thinks the cow chorus is redundant.

> *The cow sheds tears. Two great streams of water squirt*
>   *from her doleful eyes.*
> *Enter a dancing chorus of cows.*

So we cut it. Though I will miss this stage direction:

> *Andrew Lloyd Webber was close with* Cats *but he*
>   *missed the full Broadway potential of dancing cows.*
>   *Not so our brave choreographer, who has a chance*
>   *for a dance that will be a four-legged terpsichorean*
>   *extravaganza.*

Later I realize I was trying to get the girls onstage for the finale to act 1, so I must reintroduce them as fishnet-stockinged French hookers or perhaps that shiny French raincoat look.

Mike suggests that when the cow is launched on the British, it explodes.

"Like a nuclear cow?" I suggest and we toy with having them collapse to the ground and then begin to click their coconuts to build up the rhythm for "Run Away." This could be quite effective. It could also be pretentious and quite horrible, but I'm sure we will find that out early enough.

Another great line from Mike: "It is not overinteresting."

He is the master of the understatement.

One of the best ideas is that the Lady of the Lake will bring Galahad back onstage in the Gilliam dragon boat, but while they sing their duet "The Song That Goes Like This," the boat will slowly start to sink, so they will sink with it. I think this should be hilarious. The Lady goes down with the ship and has disappeared by the end. I think this is both mad and inspired in the best Pythonic tradition.

The really encouraging aspect of these meetings is that everyone in the room is so talented and filled with ideas, enthusiasm, and solutions. Hugh Vanstone is highly valuable; and we all recognize this instantly and insist on continuing our meeting until five thirty since his time is scarce (he is opening *Bombay Dreams* this Thursday).

Mike wants snow falling in the auditorium and I say that I love it, but the only way it can happen in a Python show is if it is totally inappropriate and in quite the wrong place. Like if it snows in the "Galaxy Song." Apparently there are considerable extra cost issues involved in cleaning the house after each performance to consider. We suggest perhaps it might snow at the end for "Always Look on the Bright Side of Life," which makes us giggle. This is then changed from snow to balloons.

Mike talks enthusiastically about the score and the songs, which he says "have absolutely no taste whatsoever."

John Du Prez and I roar with laughter.

Mike attempts to exit bravely by saying, "Taste, as we all know, is the enemy of the theater," but it is too late; we have our quote for our songs from him now.

These are the songs which have no taste.

SATURDAY, APRIL 24, 2004

Well, today's the day. The big read-through. I shall hobble a couple of blocks to Bergdorf Goodman on Fifth, next to our coproducer Bob Boyett's office. A guide is being sent from 101 Productions to carry my guitar. They are being cautious with the cars, and who can blame them—they have flown in all these actors from LA and stuck them in the Carlyle and other expensive hotels.

I am filled with anticipation. How will it go?

Spamalot—Reading
Saturday, April 24, 2004

Tim Curry	King Arthur
Audra McDonald	Lady of the Lake
Hank Azaria	Lancelot Villager 3 Plague Victim's Son The French Taunter Tim the Enchanter The Black Knight
David Hyde Pierce	Robin Dead Collector Villager 1 Guard 1 Black Beast Brother Maynard
Roger Bart	Galahad, aka Dennis the Mud Gatherer Villager 2 The Knight of Ni Prince Herbert's Father
Michael McGrath	Patsy Frenchie Minstrel Guard 2 Critic Policeman Soothsayer Wounded Wedding Guest
Laura Bell Bundy	Piglet Girls
Richard Easton	Historian Not Dead Yet Body God

Heather Lee	Zoot
	Dingo
	Witch
	Winston
Jim Piddock	Bedevere
	Mrs. Galahad
	Prince Herbert
	Bors

SATURDAY, APRIL 24, 2004, 5 P.M.

Well, the reading was a triumph. I felt everything worked. All the actors were hilarious. It played to continuous and very loud laughter. Going round the table introducing ourselves, David Hyde Pierce said he was terrified of reading the part of Eric Idle sitting next to the real Eric Idle.

"I'm Michael Palin," I said. . . .

It was Hank's birthday (he is forty) and they got him a cake, which was touching. He was hilarious in the Cleese roles, really funny, and he managed to make them his own, so that you could see a real person inside the Taunter who was enjoying winding up the English. My old pal Jim Piddock was outstanding. He could do any role in this show. Mike was also insistent that Tim Curry must be in the show and he was utterly brilliant. Well, indeed, that's why we pushed so hard for him. David Hyde Pierce was also very funny, and got several extra laughs from his delicate delivery of Sir Robin. I was pleased that many of the new gags and moments got big laughs and fit right in, without anyone noticing they are not in the film.

So at least we know the book works. Bill Haber kept trying to lead Mike into admitting that he had never heard a table read of a musical like this before, but Mike was adamant about concentrating on the concerns, and I suppose that is his job, to point out what isn't 100 percent.

I could have used a few moments of breathing in the triumph, though. Especially since at the end John and I performed "Always Look on the Bright Side of Life." He on piano, and me on guitar. It went very well. We are so used to performing this together that even separated by half the room we slipped into it effortlessly and everyone joined in lustily and then broke into tremendous applause. It was a great way to finish a table read.

The table was bestrewn with Spam cans; and at the end when we were posing for a photo of the entire team, I picked up one of the Spam cans and started pretending to take photos with it.

"Look," I said, "the Spam Cam."

Everyone thought this was a great idea: to make instant cameras out of Spam cans and hand them out.

Mike told me he was happy because he had finally discovered that the play was about something.

"It is about the English obsession with class," he said.

This was very important to him. Everything must have meaning.

Some wonderful memories of the read: Mike shaking and crying with laughter, tears coursing down his cheeks, utterly helpless at David Hyde Pierce reading Brother Maynard—"Three shall be the counting and the number of the counting shall be three. Four is right out!"—which he did brilliantly and which is an absolutely ace piece of Palin writing. The Taunter was the standout piece and almost stopped the show. I am glad I put all the Taunter bits together: it really works and will become more and more hysterical for an audience.

We had a room full of tremendously talented people, all of whom fed off one another. Roger Bart became funnier and funnier in the Michael Palin roles. There was a hilarious chap, Richard Easton, who indicated tremendous comic talent and played the Historian with great gravitas. Jim Piddock as the Mother, constantly trying to pick him up, worked a treat and paid off nicely at the end when they discover the Grail at the *Antiques Roadshow*.

All would have been copacetic if we had left it there, but afterward Mike took John and me aside and in no uncertain terms told us about all the songs he was *not* crazy about. Mike felt that every song ought to be some kind of parody of something, but it's not just *Forbidden Broadway,* surely? He most dislikes the "Lady of the Lake Song," where Arthur sings like Elvis, although this played fine. He hated the "Knights of the Round Table," and it had to be pointed out that this is a classic and from the movie and filled with visual gags and cannot easily be removed. Then he hated "Spanking," even though it has three or four quite original gags with the track sticking and the dancers sticking and then everyone going into fast forward and then fast reverse. He also disliked the new "Bring Forth the Cow!" song for which we had recorded unlikely lyrics set to Ravel's *Bolero*.

Fetchez la Vache

Fetchez la vache,
Fetchez la vache,
Fetchez la vache
Fetchez la vache (etc.)

Go fetch the cow out so we French can show how
All our taunting is an art.
In their direction we'll all fart.
So hurry now and get the cow,
So that we can show them now.

Go and fetch the beast that moos all day
While we choose some naughty words to say
Till the British run away.
You know they're gonna run away.
That's right they certainly will run run away.
They are hardly gonna stay
For our French cow.

Go and get the four-legged thing they call a cow
While we show how
This silly king
Has to go, go, go, go, go
And leave our France
While we taunt him till
He's soiled his underpants,
Till his men have run away
Back to the horrible UK,
Where French people never want to stay
Because it's fifty shades of gray
And it rains all bloody day.

So I cut it.

Which was just as well, since when John checked, Ravel was still in copyright.

The real problem with the songs is that at a table read there are live actors reading classic comedy and then they all stop while we play the CD of the music, so it is really hard to get the same appreciation for it; and when I say this and stand up for our songs, Mike says he can tell the difference.

So I felt a bit down after the triumphant read and I headed out for some punitive shopping, or "retail therapy" as John Du Prez calls it. I was trying to find something unnecessary and expensive (like *Spamalot*?), a destructive impulse to see if I can hurt my wallet! Instead I found a nice Danish tea place where I began to deconstruct my feelings.

First of all, I felt no one had actually congratulated me. Does that seem petty? Ridiculous? Of course, but I have spent two years on this script. It isn't *just like the movie.* It's seven drafts already. No one seemed to notice. It is assumed that the script is by Python and that it achieved this adaptation by parthenogenesis. No one in the room had even read the last draft, so they were laughing at new jokes for the first time.

I felt bad, no question, and I even contemplated for a moment running away back home, but I sensibly resisted. I just made some angry remarks to myself in the bathroom, slammed some loose change around the room, and then called my wife and daughter. After that I called John Du Prez, who *had* received all the praise and congratulations of everyone, which he relayed, and that cheered me up. So it was all okay again. . . .

SUNDAY, APRIL 25, 2004, 7:30 A.M.

I find I am a pessimist by night but an optimist in the morning, and I awoke in a much better frame of mind. Positivity returns. Yesterday afternoon I went out with Steve and Anne Martin. We picked up Stella McCartney in the Village in a limo and went to the de Kooning opening at the Gagosian Gallery and afterward had dinner at the Odeon. Traffic was insane and we sat for an hour in the limo, just gassing and laughing, quite agreeably, as we circled the West Village.

We didn't stay long at the gallery looking at the huge, highly colored squiggles.

"From his insane period," Steve informs me, "that's why everyone thinks they are not so good but I think they are brilliant."

His only regret is that he sold his two. Bought for $150K, sold for $850K. Now they are worth millions. They estimate these on the wall as two and a half million each. I think I can do without.

Jerry Seinfeld joins our table at the Odeon. He is a big Python fan. He has just returned from Daytona driving very fast cars with Derek Bell, and he looks happy and relaxed. His wife is adorable, raven haired and with an unusual big circular diamond in a pendant around her neck.

"I'm not really a diamond girl," she said, which reduced Stella McCartney to hysterics. Stella is a hoot—hilarious and vivacious and very honest. I liked her immediately. She was recently married. She is also related to half the room through her mum, and knows all this rather posh crowd from growing up summering in the Hamptons. Johnny Pigozzi is there with his funny and friendly Greek girl.

New York continues to be New York. It still remains the only city in the world where you can get the Sunday papers on a Friday.

I managed to make a grumpy cabby laugh pointing out a woman standing in shorts shaving her legs in the fountain outside the Plaza. The cabdriver said, "Only in New York," in that ambivalent way New Yorkers do. Leaving you in doubt to as whether they are actually boasting or apologizing.

NEW YORK, SECOND WEEK

THURSDAY: I work at Icarus with Mike, Casey, and John Du Prez.

FRIDAY: More notes and I begin rewriting act 2 at Icarus.

SATURDAY: I'm still rewriting act 2 at the Essex House hotel.

SUNDAY: I finish rewriting act 2. Not for the last time!

MONDAY: Morning meeting with John at Bob Boyett's office. At noon we go over to Mike's office for the model meeting with Tim Hatley— we're there till 4.

TUESDAY: Casey, John, and I work at Bob Boyett's office and we're joined by Mike.

WEDNESDAY: I rewrite in the hotel in the morning. A meeting at Mike's round the corner (Icarus). In the afternoon we record three songs with John.

In the last seven days it seems we have rewritten a whole musical: tightening, shaping, and deepening. I've written three completely new songs, four segments of songs, and sharpened endless lyrics. We've done several middle sections, B sections, and C sections. Even I am impressed by the work achieved. Not just by me, I hasten to add. Casey, John, and Mike have probed and prodded and patiently laughed at my one-liners.

Mike has been constantly nudging us for B sections and C sections in our songs. He seems very knowledgeable musically as well. He often refers to his pal Stephen, who is, naturally, Sondheim, whom he has known for forty-six years.

"Who knew he was the Mozart," he says, "while Lenny was only the Salieri?"

Lenny is Bernstein, no less.

John and I work fast. We take a hint of melody and a few lines and turn them into a moment. Our goal on these rewrites is to find little reference points to other musicals. We managed to make the new mud song not only a revolutionary *Les Mis* song but also put in a sly reference to *South Pacific*.

"What do you put a clean white suit for?"

"Mud."

The "Mud Song" is new. It will be cut. "Don't Laugh at Lancelot" is new. It will be cut. "He's Different," which Tim Curry originally recorded back in LA with the wonderful Julian Sands, now has a whole new set of lyrics and is in act 2 where it should be hilarious. It wasn't and it won't be, as it, too, was cut.[*]

---

[*] However, it did end up in *What About Dick?*, still sung by Tim in his role as the Reverend Whoopsie.

"A Spanking Tonight." We've cut this down, reordered it, and now there's a full *Amadeus* chorus where the Anthrax Castle prisoners come on as eighteenth-century fops. We thought that would be hilarious, but we could never persuade either Mike or Casey that the Castle Anthrax scene should remain in the play; and despite three different songs that we demoed, they and it were always cut.

The Knights of Ni song has been rewritten and there's now a whole new bridge. More Disney than anything, it still sank without trace. The Lady of the Lake song has a whole new bridge. It won't save it. "Run Away" has been shortened and rewritten and we go into the interval much faster and quicker and tighter. We still have vestigial traces of "I'm Not Dead Yet," but the "Mud Song" has been cut.

One triumph: "I'm All Alone," a new song which came to me walking down the street.

The gag just popped into my head, and I realized it was funny, and I turned right round and went straight back to the Essex House hotel, where I wrote the lyrics and music, on the nice Taylor guitar 101 have kindly bought for me. When lost in the forest in act 2, Arthur sings "I'm all alone" to Patsy, whose puzzled face will reveal to us exactly what he is thinking. I like the gag because it's entirely up to the actor playing Patsy to let the audience know when to laugh. The tune I wrote was fairly soon brilliantly replaced by John Du Prez. I was reminded of what he did to the "Galaxy Song" in

The Meaning of Life movie. Now this song, too, has a wonderful melody. I think it will play.

It does. And it stays.

After a long exhaustive meeting in Bob Boyett's office on Tuesday, I asked Mike what his next appointment was. He looked around, slightly panicking.

"I don't think I have one," he said anxiously.

"In that case," I said, "we must go to lunch."

And Mike enthusiastically led the way to a curbside trattoria, where we ate spectacular Italian food.

Over lunch Mike told a great anecdote about Sheldon Harnick, the lyricist of *Fiddler on the Roof.* He had been home for a few weeks and one night he said to his wife, "You know, darling, it's been so peaceful, so nice being home like this."

And she said, "For your information, for the last two weeks I have not been speaking to you. . . ."

That afternoon Mike wanted us all to attend an audition at the Shubert Theatre.

Obviously Monty Python was an all-male group, and so apart from adding the essential chorus ladies singing and dancing, we have created a great new leading role for a mezzo-soprano. The character is taken from a brief speech in the movie by King Arthur about the Lady of the Lake, who has legitimized his role as king: "The Lady of the Lake, her arm clad in the finest samite, held aloft Excalibur, to show that I, Arthur, was your king!"

In the film we never see her, she remains firmly off-screen, so we created a new role for an African American diva to add a great singing voice and some female comedy into the play. At the read Audra McDonald kindly read the character for Mike, but at this point there is no real part there at all and no one is surprised when she declines. Since then, Mike has steadily been auditioning divas. Now he is very excited.

"Does she *have to be* African American?" he asks.

"No. I just think we need a great voice."

"Could she be Hispanic?"

"Absolutely."

That afternoon we sit expectantly in the Shubert, Mike, Casey, me, Bill, Jeff Wilson, Wendy Orshan, and John. There is a little light on the stage as we take our places in the empty auditorium.

"We're ready," says Wendy, mindful of the million things Mike has to do.

Peter Lawrence brings onto the stage a young dark-haired woman and introduces Sara Ramirez. She begins to sing something by Sondheim. Instantly we are transfixed. It is magical. The power of her voice commands everyone's attention. It seems to come from deep inside her. In an instant we are all won over. I have never seen a singer with so much control or such hold over her listeners.

We all turn to Mike.

Wow!

We have our Lady of the Lake.

WEDNESDAY, APRIL 28, 2004

After a day's writing in my loft in the Essex House, I'm walking around in my underpants, typing, feverishly writing songs, writing scenes—it's like a cliché from some old classic movie. The writer holed up working on a Broadway musical. Sadly, I'm in so much pain that I have to leave the hotel and go down to the nearest pharmacy and buy myself a wrist support and an elbow support and a shoulder support because I'm just aching. And yet I am very happy with the way things are going. I am most pleased with the way things have fallen into place with the characters. Lancelot now starts off as an angry man with a whole new song called "Don't Laugh at Lancelot." His story evolves into a surprisingly happy ending with Prince Herbert, when he finally comes out of the closet. This, too, was based on a hint in the movie. At the end of the Castle Anthrax scene when Lancelot is helping Galahad to escape from Zoot and the temptation of the ladies he says:

Galahad: Couldn't I have just a bit of temptation?
Lancelot: No.
Galahad: Oh, I bet you're gay. . . .

Adapting the movie with ninety-eight speaking roles into a stage play, I combined as many parts as I could that were originally played by the same Python, wherever possible making them *aspects* of the same character, or earlier stages in their lives. For instance, Lancelot (Lance) starts off as a guard bickering about swallows. He sets off to join King Arthur's army with his pal Robin, also a guard and a fellow ornithological fanatic. We will discover and reveal, through the course of rehearsals and endless rewrites of act 2, that Lancelot's anger and violence turn out to be based on a lie he is living about his own sexuality. He is repressing something that when he accepts it will change his life.

Michael Palin's constitutional peasant Dennis also reveals his unhappiness with life, living with his mum, mining mud, having to be filthy all the time, while he rigorously criticizes the major social problems of the day. He jumps eagerly into a new state of cleanliness once he has been "converted" by the Lady of the Lake. He becomes Sir Dennis Galahad. In the current draft, despite being severely tempted by Zoot, he will resist the Sirens and end up with the Lady of the Lake. That's the story so far. It may change.

And thankfully we have found our Lady of the Lake. The magnificent Sara. A major talent of epic proportion whose effect on everyone was mesmeric. Her deep, rich contralto voice spoke across the ages. Her precise diction. Her high intelligence. Her sexual appeal. She is a goddess. She will be brilliant and a huge star.

The plot is now simple. King Arthur, with the assistance of a diva in a pond, has proclaimed himself king and set off to round up some knights, to take them to Camelot, where God himself gives them a Quest, to seek and find the Holy Grail.

"God, the Almighty and all-knowing, has misplaced a cup?"

A *SPAMALOT* COMPANY DINNER

THURSDAY, APRIL 29, 2004

A dinner for forty people in a private room at Sparks restaurant. A mob victim was machine-gunned here twenty years ago and I think he was lucky to get the attention because the meal takes about an hour and a half to even get underway. There's one house waiter with a very broken nose. No one dares complain.

We've been working for days, just the four of us—Mike, Casey, myself, and John, occasionally adding Tim Hatley and Hugh Vanstone—and there are forty people in the room, all of whom have titles like executive and producer. Suddenly we feel very top-heavy. Creatively we've had a brilliant time, but there are so many people on the payroll, will any of this be spent onstage?

Bill Haber is brilliant. He makes a delightful welcoming speech, introducing everybody, and then puts me on the spot when he says he has the most respect for writers.

"They sit in a room," he says, "with an empty piece of paper and then suddenly all you people are employed!"

Laughter.

Now I have to get up and make an impromptu speech. I thank Bill, of course, adding, "My ideas would be nowhere, without him picking it up and paying for it all."

I also thank Mike. "It's the best job I've ever had."

"Welcome to the top table," says Mike.

Bill Haber continues to impress us as the most brilliant and thoughtful producer ever anywhere. He even pops over to Iceland for the day for lunch with the prime minister in an effort to stop them slaughtering whales. Mike is, as I am, totally respectful of his amazing courtesy and courtesies that extend in every direction.

Spam is apparently interested in my idea of the Spam Cam. . . .

FRIDAY, APRIL 30, 2004

Mike began a meeting yesterday with a forty-minute speech about what was wrong with my script. It was in front of everyone and it felt very unfair to me. He set off on a long, rambling, and to me never-ending moan that quickly turned a packed, optimistic meeting into a room full of puzzled people, staring silently at the carpet.

He cannot work, he says, unless he knows the subtext. There are eleven hundred Jews waiting to pounce. What if they are angry about what has been done to their favorite classic? Our show must have *some* of the Broadway elements, and every show on Broadway has some underlying secret—we don't know what it is, but it must have it. It doesn't show, but it is an underlying thread. This was interspersed with references to Jerome Robbins and shows long gone. We even had an example from *Annie*.

I sank lower and lower into my chair and plunged further and further into gloom. I hate this. This is precisely what depresses me—some vague, rambling anxiety that lacks any specificity. How does one go about correcting that? After all, I did work in a fairly successful writing group for a few years and some of our lads were not afraid of a good row, but we had principles of engagement: no rhetoric, no speeches, always it's *this* suggestion versus *that* suggestion. Winner takes all. Best idea never too late. Good Oxbridge principles. From the mid-fifteenth century. But with Mike's monologue I'm not even sure I understand what it is he is saying that I am missing. *Subtext?* In Monty Python?

When he finally finished speaking, nobody said a word for about a minute and then John, bless him, bravely spoke up for me and staunchly defended my script. Challenged, Mike instantly reversed himself.

"The songs are parody," he said.

"No, they are not just parody," I argued, feeling a little heat circulating at last. Finally I was remembering a Python lesson I had to learn over the years: If you don't speak up for yourself, nobody will listen.

" 'The Song That Goes Like This' *is* a kind of sui parody. It is a song about itself, that makes fun of itself, and of Broadway songs in general. It isn't just an Andrew Lloyd Webber send-up. If you want every song to be a parody, then it's *Forbidden Broadway*."

As I'm leaving the meeting, I tell Wendy I may never return. They think I'm joking, of course, but I'm not sure I am. I felt I was being publicly carpeted for something—*I wasn't sure what*—apparently something I had done wrong or had failed to do that broke some rule I was unsure of. A feeling precisely out of boarding school.

They all say to me, "Oh, it's just Mike." But this is me. I will walk into the fire if I know what it is for, but the reading was a triumph. Everyone who was in the room that day has since told me how much they loved it. Most mention they loved the music, too. I feel you start from this point and begin to improve, but Mike wants urgent work now, and I am supposed to come here and hang around in May and June and maybe July, and this has to be done before the work on the sets etc., etc.

I feel what has happened is Mike is panicking. The read was fucking hilarious—so what can he do to bring it to life onstage? He must feel the onus is on him now.

On a positive note, I did realize this morning that the Grail is essentially about the Pythons: each knight's character is a reflection of our own. Arthur, the constantly baffled; Lancelot the violent who attacks everyone and who heartlessly puts his not dead yet relative on the cart.

> Bring out your dead!
> Here's one.
> I don't want to go on the cart.
> Oh, don't be such a baby.

Galahad is sorely sexually tempted by the maidens but must resist. This is a recurring Palin trope. It reappears in *The Missionary* and *American Friends*. Then there is Terry Jones as Bedevere, the whacky theorist who reconstructs the world with his own logic, and me as Robin, the musicians' friend, who dreams of Broadway but who will run away at the first drop of danger.

So I am now, appropriately, back in the Sir Robin position. I wish to run away. I was inspired by the reaction to the read as much as I have ever been inspired. I felt justified and encouraged. After three years and seven drafts the script worked. It could be a triumph, but with Mike's anxieties—and he may very well be right—it still doesn't address what I need to hear, which is essentially "Well done, let's go get 'em."

So I am kinda angry and feel the need to stand up for myself.

Amazingly there is no need. Next morning in an extraordinary meeting Mike tearfully and wholeheartedly apologizes. He embraces me and explains it came out all wrong and he was up all night and couldn't sleep and he felt so bad and he didn't mean it to sound like that and he was truly deeply sorry and it wouldn't be like this. We can argue and disagree and we will, but it won't be like that ever again. That was wrong.

What can I say? I hugged him with tears in my eyes and explained my boarding school reactions and how with just a bit of bread and a pat on the back I'll go off and face impossible odds. So there we are. To be with Mike in this mode is just joyous. *How could I not want to work with him forever?* I am thinking. I can feel my anger and outrage softening and vanishing as the meeting progresses.

So all is well again.

PART II

—

Anxiety and Final
Rewrites Before Rehearsal

SUMMER 2004

I spent the month of May rewriting. Mike was editing his brilliant miniseries *Angels in America*. My limp turned out to be a snapped tendon in my ankle, and so in early June I had an operation and spent the rest of the summer in a wheelchair with a bright pink plaster cast. I wanted to be able to walk for our rehearsals in the fall.

Meanwhile, John and I work on more songs at what we now call Killer Rabbit Studios on Ventura Boulevard. They have even put a neon sign up for us. Sara Ramirez and Tim Curry join us, adding their voices to our demos. We come up with another "Spanking" song. It will meet the same fate as its predecessors.

Mike always takes August off for a summer break on Martha's Vineyard. In early September he is joined by Casey. I am still immobilized, but Tania drives me around Utah with my leg up in the back of a gold Lexus with Lily riding shotgun.

SUNDAY, SEPTEMBER 5, 2004

Mike calls from the Vineyard. He is relaxed and friendly. He has Casey with him. They are working for a few days. Sounds good. But as he reveals what they are doing my heart sinks. They seem not to be just working on the dances and the transitions between scenes. It seems they have had some "great ideas for the play." One he lets me have briefly. They have agreed that there are no great numbers in act 2 (?) and they want to end act 1 on "Find Your Grail" and boot the next two numbers into act 2. My heart sinks. Oh no. He will call me tomorrow with the details.

I have a sleepless night. I have now spent ten drafts finding the best shape, and the best act break, and after a couple of days with the choreographer, Mike wants to change it. It makes no sense to me. Act 2 is already way too long. If he cuts it the way he proposes, he is going to end up with a forty-minute first act and an act 2 of two and a quarter hours.

The French Taunter is clearly the comedy climax of act 1, and we have to send them into the bars for intermission, still laughing at that. The plot is simple: the French taunting causes the British knights to run away, to flee for their very lives. The English are utterly dispersed and King Arthur starts act 2 all alone (apart from Patsy) in a dark and very expensive forest. Now he must somehow find his knights and then seek the Holy Grail.

I am so anxious I wake up at four. After wrestling with my thoughts for an hour, I call John Du Prez in England and we have a long talk. Is it normal, I wonder, for the choreographer and the director to rewrite the book? After my long talk with John, I realize I have to speak up and defend my text. There is only a month to go and we can't start ripping apart the work of three years. If only we can try what we have first, I don't mind changing anything afterwards, but this feels like panic.

I haven't had any comments at all from Mike on my new script that I rewrote in May after they gave me all their notes. I simply don't know what he thinks about the current book. I got neither a call nor an email from him about it, or any of the new songs we sent. We arrange a conference call to discuss all this. It lasts an hour and a half. At the end I have lots of notes. Mike and Casey have an idea of Arthur at the end of a long table and he only gets the idea for the knights of the *Round* Table at the end of the dance, when he goes to Vegas, ends up in his underpants broke, and then sings "I'm All Alone." I hate it so bad I can't keep my mouth shut. I have to say why I feel it is a bad idea. The "Knights of the Round Table" is a classic Python bit—you can't just have them sing "We're knights of the long table." In any case. John and I tried this all before when we were starting off and we even wrote a song for it. . . .

What Shape Shall Arthur's Table Be?

The universe's a marvelous thing.
It's made entirely out of string
And everything, and all you see

Comes from a tiny wrinkly pea.
But one thing still obsesses me
When we sit down to take our tea.
How can we sit down equally?
What *shape* shall Arthur's table be?
Shall it be oval, cubed, or square,
Rectangular, triangulare?
Shall it be T-shaped? Like a Vee?
What shape shall Arthur's table be?

Should it be pointed like a star?
A long line like a sushi bar?
Clam shaped, ham shaped, like a tree?
Or perhaps a table shaped like me?
Should it be something like a duck
Or like a toad? No, that's bad luck.
How can we sit down twenty-three?
What shape shall the damn table be?
Shall it be oval, cubed, or square,
Rectangular, triangulare?
Shall it be B-shaped, like a bee?
What shape shall Arthur's table be?

Elliptical or like a tube?
Oblong? Pear-shaped? Like a cube?
Hollow like the letter P?
Or F? Or Y? Or G? Or C?

Rhomboid, ovoid, diamond shape?
A flag? A bag or like a drape?
Egg shaped, something like a pig,
Or elephant? No, that's too big.
To avoid all jealousy
Everyone should sit near me.
The perfect shape it must be found.
The shape of the table should be . . .
Something very dear to me,
Something very near to me,
Something over there I see,
Something just behind the tree. . . .

[*They see the moon.*]
That's it!
The moon's the answer, I'll be bound!
The perfect table shape is found.
King Arthur's knights shall be renowned
For dining at the Table Round!

In the end John and I came to the conclusion that, as it wasn't that funny, we should just buy the myth and not start playing about with it, because we'll weaken it if we make jokes about just everything. They listen and move on. I think it is a good conversation; we have some areas of agreement. I understand their concern for a big dance number in act 2. Sadly neither of them likes "Spanking" at all.

"Who *are* these girls?" worries Mike. "What are they doing there?"

How do I answer such a question? Later I ask my daughter.

"Who are the girls of Castle Anthrax?"

"It doesn't matter," she says. "They're funny. . . ."

Well quite.

Mike calls later in the day and we talk for another hour and a quarter. He is very concerned. He has never experienced this, someone so resistant to his ideas, even when he wrote with Elaine May. I say I have never worked with a director who didn't tell me what he thought of the script or let me have any notes. What am I supposed to do—*intuit* how he feels? We are both very forthright.

"You and I have been friends for a long time," he says, "but I don't see how I can go on."

I don't back down.

"I don't see how I can go on if the choreographer and you are allowed to pull to bits the structure of the show that I have worked on for three years, without giving it a go."

We have both shown each other the door. He'll walk, I'll walk. It feels better.

We discuss more details. I think I succeed in making it clear that I am not against his ideas at all, far from it, but I must resist things I think are wrong or less good than what we already have. I also say I need to hear a lot more about what *he* thinks about the text. I explain the plot of act 2 again, how the English are scattered and lost and Arthur must regain his knights. That's why "I'm All Alone" works where it is: it comes out of a real emotion, his anxiety that his quest is failing and he has lost everyone. Mike says he didn't realize that, I hadn't made this clear in the text. I think it's there, but I promise to emphasize it. I think he understands my plea to keep the act break where it is.

The main issue seems to be there is no big production number for dancing in act 2: there are smaller numbers and cabaret numbers and quartets. But act 2 has an awful lot of funny stuff in it. The big dance number we wrote was "A Spanking Tonight," but both Mike and Casey are very coy about it. Tim Hatley gets it completely and I'm convinced the audience will love it, but Broadway anxiety is everywhere. They seem unconcerned about Chicago—it's all about what the New York critics will think. It paralyzes people and they rush to find bad solutions to problems that don't exist.

Still, and most importantly, Mike and I patched up our relationship. I feel good that I said what I think, and I stood up for my writing. It felt like good therapy to me. I hope it was good for Mike, too, and we're not heading for a Garry Shandling relationship. Perhaps all will be healed. We promise to stay in touch and talk. I guess we'll see.

SUNDAY, SEPTEMBER 19, 2004

Mike is out here for the Emmys and is everywhere with his utterly brilliant cast and writer of the miniseries *Angels in America*. They deservedly sweep the board, winning eleven awards.

> **56th Prime-Time Emmy Awards**
> Outstanding Miniseries: *Angels in America*
> Outstanding Directing for a Miniseries: Mike
> Nichols

MONTECITO

FRIDAY, SEPTEMBER 24, 2004

Well, what a difference three weeks makes. Things couldn't be better. After Mike and I had our talk, things immediately improved. There was much to-ing and fro-ing of phone calls and emails with people letting each other know what they were doing and what their concerns were. This became so healthy that the meetings with Casey, Mike, and John at our LA home last week were a virtual lovefest. We discovered that not only were we all on the same page but that it was an illuminated manuscript.

The meetings began with Casey and Glen Kelly (our

piano dance arranger) playing through the various numbers as we ran through the text. Glen is an extraordinarily fine player and John and I were both thrilled with his arrangements of "Mud" and "Burn Her." In fact, most of the music was well received, even the shocking news that the "Critic Song" had shifted into the minor key. I wrote it as a sort of Noël Coward number, but now they have switched it into *Fiddler on the Roof*. Mike says for him this removes all the stigma from the number and there will be a great Tevye moment for David Hyde Pierce. I suggest that since David is also a concert pianist he should actually play live, great big Rachmaninov arpeggios, which Glen immediately ran to the piano and performed. Very impressive he was, too. Everyone liked this idea.

There was a little tension around the still missing big number in act 2. John and I had worked on a long and what I thought was a funny intervention by the pope and his cardinals, but when we played it for them, Mike and Casey did not like it at all. They also remained adamantly opposed to the "Spanking" number. I listened hard and suddenly came up with an idea. Since we are going into "He's Different" anyway, what if *that* thought now leads into the big number in act 2 and it's all about Lancelot and whether indeed he might be gay. Instant unanimous enthusiasm all round for this idea and I improvised a sort of Peter Allen "Rio" number:

His name is Lancelot.
He wears tight pants a lot.
He likes to dance a lot and dream.
No one would ever know
That this outrageous pro
Bats for the other team.

During the number Lancelot will be transformed into an outrageous costume. We will watch him come out. This could be an hilarious moment for Hank. First he is puzzled, then in denial, then he gradually comes round. And out. We all love this idea and I created the lyrics overnight. John took no time setting them to a spanking tune. Well, not *spanking* obviously, but Casey now has a great dance number in act 2 to work on. Mike said the lyrics were great and he loved the whole song. For our plot this now sets up a romance between Lancelot and Prince Herbert, whom he has just rescued.

Lancelot: I thought your son was a lady.
Father: I can understand that.

John and I had a few minor grumbles over the cutting of King Arthur's song about the Lady of the Lake, which I personally loved, but I think Mike has a point: it is too relaxed and lacking in grandeur for the first appearance of our diva, the Lady of the Lake. In fact, after a long talk with Tim Hatley, I realized that this is going to be a great stage moment and we really don't need another song before "The Song That Goes Like This." So we cut it.

The other song we cut was the "Knights of Ni." This is a song we have dicked about with quite a bit but have never particularly solved. Ours is far too Disney. No one likes it. Casey and Glen Kelly played their version, which was frankly not good either; and so after a few minutes I suggested we cut the number since it wasn't doing anything and simply move on to Sir Robin. This seemed like a good idea and that's what we have gone with.

One of the most useful ideas was when I finally realized (duh!) that the Lady of the Lake should end up with King Arthur, and not Sir Galahad. It is far more appropriate and it works a treat, especially now she tells him her real name.

King: Wait, I can't just call you Lady. Do you have a name?
Lady: Everyone has a name, Arthur.
King: What is yours?
Lady: My name . . . is Guinevere!
Robin: Holy shit!

So with great food, great weather, and our great house to work in, it was a lovefest. Mike's miniseries had become the most awarded at the Emmys, everybody loved him, he had been thanked royally by everyone, so he was beaming and happy.

PART III

—

New York
Rehearsals Begin

MONDAY, OCTOBER 18, 2004

We're up and running. I flew into NY for the start of rehearsals for *Spamalot*, sad as usual to be leaving home.
Packing, saying farewell to wife and child. Off to boarding
school for the new term. Tomorrow is our first cast read.

The first person I meet at the airport is Brooke Shields,
a tall attractive woman following a tottering angel in pink
between the wide aisles of airport seats.

"That's my baby," she yelled at me, pointing to the cute
toddler. "I'm on Broadway!"

I promised to go see her.

On my way to the first cast read, passing Times Square, a
middle-aged woman recognized me.

"*Ni*" was all she said!

Into our rehearsal rooms on 42nd Street, a very clean new
rehearsal facility. We have two studios, the largest of which
is entirely mirrored on one wall while the other wall has
huge twenty-foot windows overlooking 43rd Street. It is
currently packed with expectant producers. The actors are
downstairs at an Equity meeting.

Eventually the players arrive. There is a general jollying of the atmosphere. We sit around in a big circle.

"All right, everyone, introduce yourselves and tell us what you do," says the very dapper suited Bill Haber.

At least sixty people outline what they do.

It finally gets to me.

"Eric Idle," I say. "Job creator."

Big laugh.

There are T-shirts for all.

"This show is all about swag," I say, pouncing.

Finally we get the producers out of the room. Then we get to the read. There are huge laughs, right from the top. Tim Curry is brilliant as King Arthur, his pacing magisterial and his timing regal. The exchange about the coconuts has to pause for continued and prolonged laughter. Alongside Tim, Michael McGrath as Patsy is very sweet and charming and funny.

The cheerleaders get a big laugh, and then "The Song That Goes Like This" plays really well, even though it is only performed by John and me. Sara, who has so far been reluctant to sing and has let me take her roles in the songs, finally comes to my rescue in the "Cow Song" and blows me away. She is hilarious as Marlene Dietrich.

Hank as the Taunter is ridiculously funny. He is already off book.

"I have been doing it since I was fifteen," he explains.

The new Shakespeare/Kennedy/Churchill/Arthur speech plays to big laughs. It is totally new material and really works. Tim kicks the shit out of it, nailing every line. Act 1 shoots by.

"Sixty-five minutes," says our tall, saturnine stage manager, Peter Lawrence.

There is only one slow moment: "Don't Laugh at Lancelot." Maybe it's because only John and I and the music department are singing, but it doesn't go off at all well. Mike and I mark it for later.

"It's for David and Hank," I say. "Let's wait until they try it."

Huge cheers and applause after the reading of act 1. Everyone has big smiles on their faces as there is a general race for the toilets. A happy and noisy men's room. They let me go first! There's a new courtesy for you. . . .

Act 2 starts off really well. Hank as the Knight of Ni is inspired. Tim is very funny with him. Sara gets applause for "Whatever Happened to My Part?" She has the ability to switch into a higher gear when performing, which simply demands your attention and admiration. She totally knows how to work an audience. My concern that this song wouldn't work now that she is playing not just the Lady but also the Cow and the Witch was unfounded. It works. What didn't work was her touching scene wondering why Arthur never notices her, or rather it was really confusing moments later when she appeared again this time as Zoot. We will probably lose that character, but she will still play the Witch, and of course the Cow.

I felt the wheels came off act 2 towards the end. What Mike persists in calling "The Jew Song" didn't work. The arrangement is way too ponderous and too heavy. It kills the wit and élan of this essentially Noël Coward song. Afterwards, David Hyde Pierce agrees with me and Tim Curry also says curtly it doesn't work, so I tentatively broach the subject with Mike. There is a surprising level of agreement. I think it works from halfway in, but we discuss a much chattier opening, more Rex Harrison and less Rex Reed. Also we are going to cut the Frank Rich reference. It makes it too specific and then delivers no gag. He is no longer a critic anyway. I will be working on this tomorrow morning.

Since this song never raised the bar, the show petered out somewhat. The new ending seems intolerably long, with all the ballads being reprised and no laughs except for Herbert and Lancelot. In fact, as I point out, instead of being parody panto, it has become panto. However, there are many pluses. Christian Borle, the young man playing Prince Herbert, a newcomer to many, is quite brilliant. He is a really funny guy. In fact, the cast is impeccable. Steve Rosen is hilarious as Galahad's mother. Despite a wander across the north of England, ending up in Scotland for the accent of Doug Sills, Christian is quite benevolent and well-meaning and he draws lots of laughs. He has charm and what John Du Prez calls "a delightful swagger."

Act 2 is sixty-three minutes, which is great news. After the read, we break for sandwiches.

Mike and I discuss cutting the Black Knight—we are both in agreement on this. If it doesn't work, we'll chop it. There's still a ton of hilarious stuff. I suggest cutting Castle Anthrax, which really laid an egg. It's not Sara's fault. Mike has been saying this scene isn't funny for a year. He is absolutely right. Today it isn't even mildly amusing. This will be my first task tomorrow; but the good news is, if we only cut out the bits that didn't work at this read we will still have a hilarious show. There is so much funny stuff.

"Is that the funniest script ever?" asks a guy from the music department, as everyone staggers out. There is a general air of happiness. The ensemble, whose first day this is, look shell-shocked and excited. They are a delight on the eye.

In the afternoon, Tim Hatley entertains everyone with his toy theater, showing us the sets, which look amazing. He wins all hearts. Male and female. It is all very inspiring. And exciting.

TUESDAY, OCTOBER 19, 2004, 8:42 P.M.

An alarming swelling on my right leg reminds me I have been walking too much. Let's hope it's not a thrombosis, or these will be my final words. Thank God I pestered Tania to sign our wills before I left. It was a very depressing day, but it's about the third time I have signed a will, so at least I know it isn't terminal. Not yet. However, I am glad I have taken care of business.

I rose late for me (nine NY time) as I am still on LA hours and worked on act 2, which is concerning me. Mike is sick and stays home. A nice email concedes that the improvements to the "Critic Song" have not worked and he wants me and David Hyde Pierce to work on it. Perfect. It is a patter song; you can't suddenly turn it into *Fiddler on the Roof*.

Subj: Re: (no subject)
Date: 10/19/2004, 2:12 p.m., eastern daylight time
From: Mike Nichols
To: Eric Idle

i have stayed home to cough and retch while numbers are learned. call anytime. i am happy in my pain as i think about our show. agree about hank. but david, too, is magic. we should find more for him including if possible a number to back up jews, in case it gives out on us. what i think about the jew number is that you and david should take it back and do what you want since i believe i have taken the beginning away from what works (you, too, we all do). then we can together go on and do it with the company stuff which i believe is strong. xxoxm

I have a vague idea to cut the "Critic Song" from where it is and head sharply for the end. I outline it to John Du Prez at an early dinner at Osteria al Doge. After which, I hammer out another version of the second act and email it to 101 to be printed. I decide I will meet it at rehearsals and I'm very glad I do. The place is bouncing with joy. Casey is conducting a lovefest, showing everyone his inspired and very silly steps for "The Knights of the Round Table." I sit there with tears of laughter and a big silly grin. This is wonderful. This is what it is all about: a warm rehearsal room on a rainy day in NY. The cast and ensemble are superb. They are all really enjoying themselves.

Peter Lawrence and I walk over and look at the Shubert stage. I am concerned about one of the boxes being used for the discovery of the Grail instead of a seat in the front row. There is nothing menacing about a box, but something definitely threatening about pulling an audience member up out of the orchestra stalls. Also I think I am out of love with the Critic. I think the song should definitely be sung by Sir Robin and tomorrow morning I am going to see how that might be achieved. Peter tells me that John Cleese's secretary has called to say he will be in tomorrow. Good; he will really enjoy watching them rehearsing his song, "The Knights of the Round Table," which he wrote with Graham Chapman. My joy was so intense I wanted to email all the chaps and tell them about it. But laziness prevailed.

There was a lovely message for me from Tim Curry on my phone when I got home last night. He says he doubts he will ever be able to thank me for this. He is impeccable in this show, and that is a joy. He says modestly it's easy when the script is like this, but that's not true. The gift of timing and delivery is everything. And he has everything. David Hyde Pierce couldn't be sweeter. He, too, is concerned by the "Critic Song" and is convinced it is all about tempo. We'll get there. I am not worried.

Last night I went to the premiere of *Alfie*. A blinding shitstorm of paparazzi. A nice woman of a certain age from the *New York Post* said very charming things about me, how I was always polite and friendly with the photographers, which made me blush inwardly. She chucked me on my cheek and sent me on my way.

The after-party was at TAO, where I saw Michelle Manning for the first time in a long time—since the old Dominick's days—and Sean Daniels, who are the producers. I circulated and hung with Dave Stewart and Anoushka and Gina Gershon and Mick Jagger, who slid in for a kiss. It's very nice to see him again. He asked if he could come to the *Spamalot* opening in March, which was very sweet. My old friend Lorne Michaels was there and invited me to come and watch Jude Law doing *SNL* on Saturday. Maybe.

The party emptied suddenly, like a stand at a rainy Wimbledon.

Subj: Re: (no subject)
Date: 10/19/2004, 7:31 p.m., eastern daylight time
From: Mike Nichols
To: Eric Idle

i will be in in the morning, too, of course. can't wait to see
what casey is doing. i agree about act 2 and we will talk.
there is nothing we can't fix. it is just so funny and so
intelligent. like you. Xoxxm

WEDNESDAY, OCTOBER 20, 2004, 10:22 P.M.

A rather wonderful day. Mike was going on again about the
perfidious people who keep theatrical diaries. I didn't fess
up. Should I? I don't think so. It's not like I'm intending to
publish it. He also rather scarily began to talk about Gower
Champion and the perfect way he died on the opening night
of his show, thereby ensuring it was a hit.

I said the price was too high. Couldn't he just get sick a
little?

Mike laughed heartily, but I must have jinxed him because he is now sick and was coughing all night. I think he
was freezing as we sat together in a super-cooled Ambassa-
dor Theatre, watching the tenth-anniversary production of
Sondheim's *Passion*. Two hours without an intermission.
What is it about Broadway? Do they not have bladders?

Anyway, it's worrying that Mike is sick, but fortunately he comes in to take his place at the table next morning.

He apologizes for being slightly late.

"It was crazy traffic," he says. "The whole of the Upper East Side was total Yidlock."

Collapse of writer. He smiles to himself. He got me. We sit beside each other, with our backs to the huge mirror wall. The dancers perform in front of us looking at a double image of us, front and back. But of course everyone is looking at themselves.

The great news of the day was the visit of John Cleese, which couldn't have been better timed. Or nicer. We hugged and embraced and it was really sweet to see him. He walked in just as they were rehearsing the "Knights of the Round Table," the song he wrote with Graham, and he couldn't have been human and not delighted. As it was, the ensemble saw him and perked up and performed the life out of this really funny number. He was amazed and delighted that this was only the second day of rehearsal. He was affable and charming and happy. We then watched and howled together as they learned "Finland," which is going to be a hilarious opening number. Casey is magic. His infectious humor and sense of fun pervade the dance studio. John left after saying he'll be back next Monday to record the voice of God.

Mike thinks the billing should read: And John Cleese as God.

We also rehearsed the opening and the coconuts. Tim is

really funny. He comes in like Ian McKellen and goes straight over the top. A real bravura panto performance. David and Hank are very sharp and very funny. Of course, they are TV actors, used to getting it right quickly. Mike asked us to cut "Don't Laugh at Lancelot." We are going to discuss it tomorrow, but it seems sensible. We flagged this cut on day one. You simply cannot have two numbers together.

I'm a little anxious about the changes I made in act 1 today, but am old and wise enough to know that I must leave it until tomorrow morning to read in the cold light of day. Or predawn. I started at four thirty this morning. There simply is no stopping the subconscious when in writing mood. I'm struggling hard with act 2. It's nice to have something to obsess about, but I don't want to bathwater-and-baby it. I am optimistic we did some good work today.

THURSDAY, OCTOBER 21, 2004

No wonder they call it the city that never sleeps. It's too damn loud to sleep. I am woken in the night by the blaring, constipated honking of an emergency vehicle, the one o'clock clatter of the garbage trucks, and then again at six by an incessantly wailing ambulance siren, which seemed to be right outside my window although I am eighteen floors up. In the street the honking of the cabs can make you leap out of your skin. I noticed once before that even the birds here shout. I miss the city that never wakes. . . .

Today was the most flattering day of my working life. They read through the changes of act 2 and there were tears of joy in people's eyes. Glen Kelly said, weeping, he had never seen anything like it. They couldn't believe the speed it had been done and they adored the changes. Casey, too, was incredibly flattering and Mike squeezed my arm and afterwards hugged me. They love the new order, so I can die a happy man. They said it was breathtaking. Now that the Knight of Ni gives King Arthur the insane task of mounting a Broadway musical, Robin can sing what was once the "Critic Song." Now his whole character falls into place. He is a man who loves musicals; he has minstrels: "That is what we do in the evening." He is also the Guard in act 1, a simple security guard with the task of removing the bodies of plague victims, who dreams of becoming a real knight with his pal Lance, who will soon become Sir Lancelot.

Well, gotta go bring out the dead.

Oh, I got one for yer.

MONDAY, OCTOBER 25, 2004

As promised, John Cleese came in on the following Monday, down from Cornell, to record the voice of God. Interestingly he was an hour late, which made Mike a little unhappy, which he covered effortlessly.

John said, "He who is late gives people plenty of time to talk about their faults."

Tim Curry, who was kept waiting at the studio, didn't look overjoyed but was very polite to his new landlord. John has cunningly sublet his New York apartment to him for the run of the show. He himself forestalled all potential criticism for tardiness by announcing he had just nearly been killed. Now, there's an entrance. He was being driven down from Cornell in a limo and had been asleep for about an hour when he suddenly woke up and saw that they were heading off the road. He saw his driver falling asleep. He yelled twice loudly and the guy woke up and pulled them back a foot from disaster, where they would both have been killed. This is an alarming story, chilling and scary, and only later do we realize that it happened at dawn that day and did not explain why John was so late. However, it is a joy to see him back in the studio; and as he runs the lines with Tim, he is hilarious. We don't quite match that first feeling on the taping, but it is close. He tenses a little for the actual recording, but still his God has a wonderful testiness about him.

"Of course, it's a good idea. I'm God, you fucking tit!" he ad-libs.

We also do a more usable one, though I love a swearing God and that will be one we will use for years (at a very reasonable charge of course).

Subj: (no subject)
Date: 10/28/2004, 7:42 a.m., eastern daylight time
From: Eric Idle
To: Mike Nichols

A writer called John Bennet said to me the other night that if the show contained "Always Look on the Bright Side," he would come.

I thought that was significant, so I take your point about "Bright Side."

I might be made happier if when Arthur and Guinevere come on at the end and sing their touching duet, we simply segue into "Bright Side," which I think would have the effect of bringing the audience to their feet.

I have never been with you on the bouncing ball thing, feeling that it is unnecessary—and expensively unnecessary.

In all my experiences, audiences very quickly know how to sing the single line that is the song, and most of them know it anyway.

I think we would achieve bringing them to their feet easily this way and the curtain could rise and fall while the orchestra keeps playing it, during their bows. . . .

See you at ten.

E

Subj: Re: (no subject)

Date: 10/28/2004, 7:49 a.m., eastern daylight time

From: Mike Nichols

To: Eric Idle

sounds good. especially if the cast does the verses. i do want to talk to tim about our already existing projection system for the bouncing ball, not because the audience needs it but because of the associations and gluing together that the ball can achieve. if not, not. Xxxm

THURSDAY, OCTOBER 28, 2004

The cast read through the new, new act 2; and it gets even bigger laughs as I have put in some more of the Knights of Ni, where they cannot hear *the* word—Which word? The word that the Knights of Ni may not hear—and Hank is truly and wonderfully hilarious. Sara rehearses the "Cow Song" and *is* Marlene and brilliant. She knows so much about singing, and the clichés of singers, that she is always a joy. During her wonderful cabaret reprise performance of "The Song That Goes Like This," she is upstaged, only momentarily, by a pas de deux performed by two of the men as a monk and a nun, but she fights back to capture the attention with some remarkable scat singing.

I leave for the airport a happy man.

Subj: Re: Casting/costume necessities from act 2 rewrite
Date: 10/29/2004, 4:37 p.m., Pacific daylight time
From: Eric Idle
To: Mike Nichols

It's so nice seeing my things again.

Of course it's great to see Lily and Tania, too, and
the dogs of course.

But to see my curtains and fabrics, and little things I
own, now that is worth six hours flying for.

I shall return in no time. But only if you get rid of
Bush for me.

E

Subj: Re: Casting/costume necessities from act 2 rewrite
Date: 10/29/2004, 7:11 p.m., Pacific daylight time
From: Mike Nichols
To: Eric Idle

am doing what i can about bush.

looked at the witch burning scene and liked it better
without the conversation between robin and lance on the
way to the town. it's completely acceptable that they are
new characters and also in a way the old ones, too. the
doubling and tripling and quadrupling is such a python
pleasure that it needs no linking. plus moving along fast

is another great pleasure. if you are unhappy when you
return we can keep playing. i am very happy and think
you will be, too. this is a wonderful show.

love to your curtains. don't forget to say hello to your
socks.

xxxm

Subj: (no subject)
Date: 10/30/2004, 3:39 p.m., Pacific daylight time
From: Eric Idle
To: Mike Nichols

Mike writes: moving along fast is another great pleasure
I think this is the essence of our show. . . .

Miss you but there are recompenses and not just the
curtains. . . .

E

Subj: Re: (no subject)
Date: 10/30/2004, 6:26 p.m., Pacific daylight time
From: Mike Nichols
To: Eric Idle

dollink boy,
had a very good run/stumble through the first act
today. john du prez sweetly said nice things and then that

he thought we had ruined "the song that goes like this." extreme word but true. i hadn't seen casey's staging, which was too active, too literal. easy to go back and john was perfectly right when he said lloyd weber is wooden.

2 things i took the liberty of cutting until you return and agree or dispute. one is easy—the new narration for the historian. forgive that i cannot quote but it doesn't seem to be in my script. it was short and it seemed much better just to go there without calling on the historian. the other is st. crispin's day speech. it follows the wonderful "all for one" and seems redundant and, unlike any other moment in the whole show, *trying* for laughs. it was much better without and tim felt the same.

all the rest was pretty thrilling. we have a good magic helper who showed us something very effective on tape and who will be a big help for the black knight and several of the other places.

i am more than hopeful. enjoy your freedom and being home. nothing like your own socks, huh? in their natural habitat.

xoxxm

Subj: Lord Andrew of Webber
Date: 10/31/2004, 6:21 p.m., Pacific standard time
From: John Du Prez
To: Mike Nichols
CC: Eric Idle

Dear Mike,

Eric passed on your note re "The Song That Goes Like This" and I wanted to thank you first for so graciously taking note of the ramblings of a mad old limey, and secondly for providing such a feast of invention in the rest of act 1.

I really am so thrilled with all that is going on that it seemed (and probably was) churlish picking on one section but felt I had to speak. I was most jolted by the music cuts at the end of each verse/bridge—those bars which allow the music to breathe and modulate (I hear that section of the Book of Great Songs devoted to 7-bar tunes is probably somewhat thin).

Also when Galahad now sings a rising scale to the words "It's far too high for me," it is proved beyond all possible doubt that the tune is well within his range! His voice surely needs to stick to the tune and crack, setting up the horror of upcoming modulations.

The *Titanic* reference simply lets Lord Andrew of Webber off the hook by generalizing the attack. I believe it should be a genuinely statuesque moment where all the great lord's pomposity, pretention, and, yes, woodenness are shown up. If it needs some enlivening—how about a small fan inside the bow of the boat to stream their hair? Perhaps it could go into overdrive and then break. But enough already. Thank you so much for your inspiring leadership and wonderful work. Can't wait for the revelations of next week's rehearsals.

Very best regards,
JDP

Subj: Two weeks of rehearsal
Date: 10/31/2004, 6:35 a.m., Pacific standard time
Email from Eric to the rest of the Pythons—
John Cleese, Terry Gilliam, Michael Palin & Terry Jones

I just thought you should all know that *Spamalot* is not only progressing well it is a positive blast.

I sit in a warm rehearsal room on 42nd Street watching pretty young people bending, bouncing, and stretching. And the show is pretty good, too.

In fact, I sit next to Mike with a big silly grin on my face and tears in my eyes.

I can't explain exactly the appeal—it is something to do with compounding the silliness.

John C. came in the other day just as they were

rehearsing "We're Knights of the Round Table," the song he wrote with Graham all those years ago, and he just beamed and glowed.

We then watched them doing the "Fisch Schlapping" dance and singing about Finland. Which was hilarious.

John returned a few days later to play God. And won.

His voice is now in the show.

So the reason I am writing, is to encourage you to drop by the process if you can; I think you'll find it marvelous and uplifting, and even moderately arousing.

The script, particularly act 2, was, until recently, changing daily, but it has now locked down into a better shape, and everything seems to flow, though often into unexpected quarters.

You'll see what I mean. I'll keep you updated in any case.

We have another four weeks in NY and then move to the theater in Chicago, where we just announced an extra week of performances.

Tim Curry, Hank Azaria, and David Hyde Pierce and all couldn't be funnier. Or nicer.

Mike says he hasn't been so happy since *The Graduate*.

Hugs to all.

E

Subj: Re: Two weeks of rehearsal
Date: 11/1/2004, 8:08 a.m., Pacific standard time
From: Terry Jones
To: Eric Idle
Sent from the Internet

Dear El,

Ah the magic of the theatre . . . sounds wonderful . . . warm and inviting and arousing . . . it's the girls in leotards bending and stretching that really convinces me that the whole thing is going to be a thundering success.

I wish I could get over . . . but on the other hand if Bush gets in tomorrow I think I'll give the US a miss for another four years.

I hear the extra week has sold out already—can this be true?

Fingers crossed all over my tense yet still young body.

lots of love.

Terry

Xxoxo

Subj: Re: Two weeks of rehearsal
Date: 11/1/2004, 8:08 a.m., Pacific standard time
From: Eric Idle
To: Terry Jones
Sent from the Internet

Say it ain't so, Tel.

You can't let the bastards win, and you really must see *Spamalot*—it's your creation, too.

Would a Hitler victory have stopped you going to Berlin for the ludo finals? Of course not.

Where's the man I once saw conducting a German band while stripping at a Nazi festival in Munich?

I agree anger would be a correct response, but I remain foolishly optimistic.

Remember, he is also the most hated man in America, and not just the world.

Miss you.

E

Subj: Re: Group Message
Date: 11/1/2004, 7:46 a.m., Pacific standard time
From: Bill Haber
To: Eric Idle

Eric, you're so fucking fantastic . . . but you already know
I think that, wink wink nudge nudge. Haber

PART IV

—

November in New York

WEDNESDAY, NOVEMBER 10, 2004, 6:57 A.M.

I have only a short week's break at home and then back to the fray. I awake in the Millennium Hotel to a beautiful sunrise, the Buddha-blue sky is flecked with golden bars across the Chrysler Building.

I have meetings today with people anxious to give me new jobs for nothing: a mockumentary, a website, all time-consuming, unrewarding activities. I am resolved to disappoint them. I have decided that for nothing I would much rather stay home. Is this mercenary or just sensible? I must stick to whatever I resolve, since, being British, I obviously have a weakness for the pointless gesture.

I called Tania as she was putting Lily to bed. My niece Sasha was there and my son, Carey, was downstairs and I really missed my lovely old home and its playful dogs and loving family. I warn my wife, who is coming to stay for a few days, that I have booked her a separate bedroom.

There is sadly no way, my darling, you can spend the night with me. That is cruel and unusual punishment. I have secured you somewhere nice and close for three nights. Now that it has turned cold the heating is on, and it is so dry I even woke myself with a solo variation on the trumpet voluntary. I miss you so much. After a few days without you I become cranky. I have less patience, and I am less respectful of the tortuous ego meanderings of one of the actors, whose main aim seems to have everybody watch him endlessly during rehearsals while he consistently fails to be funny. Mike looks confused and frustrated while I get cold and bitchy.

I have annoyingly realized that I am supposed to record with Seinfeld on Monday morning for the *Bee Movie*. What time is your flight?

THURSDAY, NOVEMBER 11, 2004, 1:09 A.M.

On a freezing sunny day in Union Square I spend a small fortune on a large coat. It's a beautiful, soft down Prada survival jacket that is not too hot for a 35-degree day like this. I wander around snug and warm. This should save my ass in Chicago.

Today was a good day. These days seem to be very special and very precious. Surely nothing could be as good as this in showbiz? I went to a meeting with Thomas Mygatt at Serino Coyne, our Advertising Agency, and was updated about all that is happening with our marketing and tie-ins.

The most surprising news is that Hormel is manufacturing a collector's limited edition of Golden Honey Grail Spam to mark the opening of *Spamalot*. The tin is delightfully designed with our cast in caricature and our logo and lots of very silly descriptions on the tin. This is nothing short of remarkable. A collector's edition of Spam? What a remarkable thing for a serious US business to do. I tell them that Spam is the Holy Grail of canned foods and it is now the official meat of Broadway.

Anheuser-Busch is also spending a huge sum promoting us and their Ultra brand of light beer, while Yahoo is expending up to a million dollars of promotional budget online, including hosting a mockumentary, running our ad as their first Broadway ad, and tying in with American Express to launch a new site, Yahoo on Broadway, leading off with our show. This all seems fairly incredible. I was also shown the mock-up for the front of the Shubert Theatre that will be up by the sixth of December, when we go on sale. I asked for a few changes, like a window with a cow in it. It all promises to be very exciting.

In the afternoon I went to rehearsals where they ran the opening of act 1. They had cut the "Mud Song" and there was a definite lack of a number there, and so they half-heartedly tried doing "Mud" as "Lovely Spam," but only half of it and it didn't really work; and from there the show slowly died with an endless scene between a not very funny Doug Sills and a struggling Steve Rosen.

Amazingly Mike was thrilled!

He said he'd been waiting three weeks for the show to fail, and to get to this stage. Now we could fix things. Ha ha. He is wonderful.

FRIDAY, NOVEMBER 12, 2004

We had a meeting of the Creatives (which is what they call us) in the smaller rehearsal room, with Casey, Mike, and John, where we banged around the issue of the first song and the "Mud Song" and what we are trying to do. I suggested an extended Excalibur moment, but Mike pointed out that we keep doing moments while avoiding doing numbers. Then I had a brain wave. Why not *start* with Bring Out Your Dead instead of Mud Village? That way, we move straight from Robin and Lance saying they'll get the cart to them coming on, and we can sing "I Am Not Dead Yet." Everyone leapt at this and said they loved it and gave me "that look" of awe and respect. This may work very well, since instead of the less funny scene, we can start the play off with some moments of hilarity. So I was dispatched to try it. One corollary was that the Black Knight might fall out here and, as they are spending a fortune on this effect, it raises serious questions; but back working in my hotel room that evening I didn't totally cut it. I think it might work somewhere else, and indeed it ends up very nicely in act 2, where the Black Knight can also terrorize Robin.

Late that night I emailed the new script to 101, and next morning I walked over to pick up a freshly printed copy. On my way past the Shubert Theatre two huge New York cops came over holding their fingers crossed in the air.

"Are you still on track?" they asked. "Tremendous luck, we can't wait, you're in in February, right?"

Only on Broadway can you be stopped by cops wishing you well with your play! Indeed, the whole community seems to be rooting for us, particularly the people who feed us. John and I dined once again at the Osteria al Doge. They *really* hope we stay.

MONDAY, NOVEMBER 15, 2004

Tania came into town for a few days and I was walking around with a big smile. We went to see a few plays and had some fabulous dinners. She chose an epic day to come to rehearsal, as she witnessed a rather dramatic scene. Mike greeted her with joy and sat her behind us at the table, where we were watching Doug Sills failing to be amusing with young Christian Borle as Prince Herbert.

> One day, lad, all this will be yours.
> What, the curtains?
> No, not the curtains, lad. . . .

While Doug was fine as the rather vain Sir Galahad, he could never get anywhere close to Michael Palin's Father of Prince Herbert role, neither the Yorkshire accent nor the gradually mounting frustration. He seemed only able to go straight to rage. Mike gives me a worried glance, and then suddenly and without warning Doug begins slapping Christian around. Real hard slaps, until Christian says, "Whoa, stop that! Time out."

There is a moment of stunned silence in the room.

A shocked Casey says, "Take five, everyone."

People stand around confused. What just happened? Mike walks me over to the big window for a private talk.

"What do you think?" he says.

"Well, if I work with him, I think I can help him with the Yorkshire accent," I suggest.

"No. I'm going to fire him," says Mike. "Might as well do it now."

And he does. Just like that. Takes him out to lunch and Doug doesn't return.

I love that about Mike. He doesn't tolerate anything for long. It's going to cost Bill Haber a lot to pay Doug off, but quite fortuitously we discover that Christopher Sieber, our first choice for the role, is suddenly available and by the end of the day we have a new Galahad. Chris has less than three weeks to learn three roles—Galahad, the Black Knight, and the Father—before we head off to Chicago, but his arrival makes a big difference to the cast. Tim Curry says the casting is now complete and he is going to buy himself a whole set of Louis Vuitton luggage.

Later that day Mike asks me how we are going to make the Killer Rabbit fly around the stage.

"You're the director," I say. . . .

He laughs.

WEDNESDAY, NOVEMBER 17, 2004

Mike is away for a few days in LA launching *Closer*. Sadly also Tania leaves, but I shall see her and Lily next week in Chicago for Thanksgiving. Meanwhile I work on the finale of act 2, which seems to be coming together, and soon we shall see that staged. "I'm All Alone," though splendid in itself, was sending everyone to sleep at the start of act 2, so I really needed to move it, which I did. But when we read it on Monday, that only half worked and I realized that "Always Look on the Bright Side" was wasted as an encore, so I dashed back to the hotel and worked through lunch and by about two-fifteen I had a brand-new act 2 to email over, with "Bright Side" now the opening number of act 2. Patsy will sing it to Arthur as they are both lost in a dark and very expensive forest.

I think it is a good idea to give the audience something familiar at the beginning of the second act. They have come back from the bar and they can all relax and whistle along if they want to, or have a little nap if they don't. Casey was quite right saying that it was all too ballady up front and there were no up-tempo numbers so, wonderfully, when we tried it, this rejig worked. Now "I'm All Alone" is an eleven o'clock number for Arthur.

WEDNESDAY, NOVEMBER 24, 2004

Casey and I are jubilant we have cracked act 2. We are so proud of ourselves getting it up and on its feet that, despite the actors being out all morning on a David Bailey *Vanity Fair* shoot, we finally ran it for Mike later that day. He was just back from Hollywood, and quite exhausted, and there was a little disappointment from us both that he didn't respond with total elation to the enormous changes we had made. But, of course, he was already thinking of how to improve what we now had. He had some good points to make and so, though we were close, there was still no cigar. I was about to fly to Chicago tomorrow to spend Thanksgiving with my wife, my daughter, my in-laws, and our large Chicago family, but I realized that this was my last chance to nail act 2 before the company leaves New York for Chicago, and so I made a tough decision and reluctantly canceled my travel plans. I did my best to apologize to Tania and Lily. Tania understood of course, but Lily was very sad and I felt very bad. However, I must stay and nail this script before it is too late.

THANKSGIVING DAY

THURSDAY, NOVEMBER 25, 2004

I woke up very early on Turkey Day and began work on the script. After a while I had a bright idea and called Mike and we talked it through on the phone and he liked it, so then I worked seven hours straight in my hotel room and came up with another completely new act 2. I had cards spread all over the hotel room floor and I rearranged the whole thing once again, occasionally glancing out the window as huge purple dinosaurs floated by in the street. It was the Macy's Thanksgiving Day Parade and my work all day was to the beat of marching bands.

By the evening I was exhausted but I had completed the new draft and emailed it off to 101 for printing tomorrow. Then I went to drinks at Mike and Diane's, after which we all went to a wonderful Thanksgiving dinner at the apartment of Candice Bergen and Marshall Rose, where Carly Simon sang with her son, Ben Taylor, and beautiful and very moving it was, too.

When we got our actors back on Friday morning there was considerable surprise that there was already a brand-new rewrite of act 2 for them. They read it in a circle, laughing out loud. Both Casey and Mike loved it and the actors stared at me.

You did this yesterday?

So it was all worth it; and to get me off the hook I had the whole company sign a large *Spamalot* poster, apologizing to Lily for keeping her dad during Thanksgiving, which was rushed off to Chicago. We then canceled all the planned previews for the day and set about staging the new act 2. This we completed on the Saturday; and at the end of the day we played it to an invited audience of producers and Eddie Izzard. Amazingly it worked!

They all loved act 1 (64 minutes), and they adored act 2 (55 minutes). Everyone was elated and morale was restored for heading off to Chicago. The producers were very happy. Arny Granat especially. They smell money, which cannot be a bad thing.

How to summarize six weeks of rehearsals? Amazing times, exhilarating. I have never worked so hard either. Especially this last week when I rewrote act 2 three times. I shall never forget Thanksgiving Day 2004.

And so we said a fond farewell to our New York rehearsal hall, where we have been so happy and done so much. Our company is a fighting force. They are ready to brave whatever Chicago holds in store.

Mercifully, Lily received the signed poster from all the cast, loved it, and has forgiven me.

PART V

—

December in Chicago

Coming in to the Shubert Theatre in Chicago for the first time I was impressed by the orchestra stalls filled with laptops, hundreds of people poring over computer screens. Tim the Enchanting gives a derisive sniff.

"Like fucking NASA."

Indeed.

"Not exactly panto," we agreed.

The big question for me has always been: Can you stop Broadway coming in and taking over the show and spoiling it? At first glance the answer seems to be no. Watching the opening I saw for the first time how easily it can fail. Too much dancing, too many unfunny moments. Of course things will change. That is why we are here.

Mike came in, looking much thinner after a surgery. We sit in the stalls and give notes to an exhausted Casey. I know how that is. You have been working your balls off for ten days, dealing with all the grueling lighting cues, and in come the refreshed and rested chaps instantly changing things.

My gripe, as always, is that "Finland" is not funny. Because it starts off with a dance by poker-faced people, we are not sure what is going on; and by the time they start up with the lyric about being in Finland, the laugh is quite lost. Immediately after the Historian says *England!* they must begin singing "Finland" for the gag to work. After what I thought was a triumphant rendition of "The Song That Goes Like This," which will play to huge laughs, Mike was concerned that it was all getting "too high school." He wants to bring it down. Hm. What's wrong with a nice laugh? Python never despised that. Is it the Broadway cringe? They are all scared of someone at the *Times*, whom they affect to despise but whom they quote all the time. I spoke at length about my concerns to Casey, who sweetly and wearily agreed. But it looks like he is coming down with the flu that has already claimed David Hyde Pierce. Casey could barely stand and was finally sent home early.

Bill Haber has scotched our bootleg plans. John and I had plans to release some of the first versions of songs. He intends to bribe us with a lot of money as an advance from Decca if we agree not to release our demos for six months. He threw out a six-figure amount. So I guess we take it, if it happens. There is no option anyway. It's his game and his ballpark. His very reasonable point is that after the main cast album, *then* you can put out an alternative, and he's quite right.

I seem to be hovering between optimism and pessimism. American Airlines kindly shoved me into coach from LAX to Chicago, which made me foul tempered, and I left a series of irate phone messages for poor Wendy Orshan, our company manager at 101, so that I was greeted at the airport by an abject Elie Landau, who explained that they had paid full fare but I had been stiffed by American. Fair enough—I was over my anger by then. Later there was champagne and chocolates in my room and a near hysterical message from Wendy. I felt bad for her. It was the opening night of *La Cage aux Folles*, so she was already stressed. I hope I apologized sufficiently.

I'm staying on the fifteenth floor of the Burnham, a restored building, five years a hotel, owned by a Dubliner who I met one night in the elevator. I have a two-room corner suite, modest enough but with three large windows, one side lining State Street, kitty-corner from Marshall Field's, with views down State to the lake, first a breakwater of calmer, flatter water and beyond that the varying light grays of the lake itself. Running alongside is the rumbling El, with its metal gray trains, constantly breaking like surf. The El, which defines the theater district, always thrilled and excited me. Occupying my west view is The Bean, a reflecting, shiny metal monument by Anish Kapoor, occasionally edged with snow, whose shiny, rounded surfaces reflect light from all angles, sometimes the unseen sun to the south, and sometimes the lights of moving traffic. It is always changing, always interesting, and at night it is lit up by blues and crimsons.

From my desk at the window on the north side I can see a wide expanse of undeveloped land, which was at first a tiny German Christmas village and then a beleaguered car park and then finally a bleak snowscape. On the opposite side of this empty square is the Oriental Theatre with its strange vertical advert, lit up by day and night, though its letters were never all lit up at the same time, so sometimes it exhorted *Orient* and sometimes suggested *rental*. Behind lay the great buildings of Chicago lining the river on West Wacker: the two corncob buildings, the angled splendor of the *Sun-Times* building that oriented me for days until unbelievably they began to knock it down to make way for a vile Trump monstrosity. To the right, the great Chicago Theatre, hard against the El, where I played in 2000 to three thousand people during the Chicago Comedy Festival and where Lily made her stage debut, aged nine.

The Shubert is two blocks away, a freezing trot in bad weather, a store-hugging dash in the rain, an ice-avoiding street-hugging run in trepidation during the melting days of falling ice. The currently heavily scaffolded theater is a two-thousand seater, like so many on my tour, a four-tiered hulk: the deep, wide orchestra stalls, with seats spreading back under the small shelf of the loge; propped up by pillars. Here, under a similar shelf, lies the mezzanine, a steeply angled section; and above that, reached by angled stairways and constant climbs, the nosebleed balcony, from whence will come great cheers and shouts of recognition.

SATURDAY, DECEMBER 11, 2004, 11:01 A.M.

It's coming alive. You can feel it. Great surging chunks of optimism. Sudden cloudbursts of laughter. The cast is bonding. Being away from Broadway helps, and the weather helps. It's like an out-of-town movie. We have three major snowfalls bringing traffic to a standstill and leaving us scurrying between buildings avoiding the falling ice.

Sadly, sickness lurks in the wings. There is still no David Hyde Pierce, and Sara is coughing and not sleeping. But there is always someone to step up. The cast is magnificent. They are tireless and patient as stock. They sit on the stage calmly while lights are moved or cues are re-cued. Bit by bit and step by step we got to the intermission tonight. I left Mike relighting Witch Village. He has all the dedication of a great film director. The genius is in the detail. I prefer the broad stroke and the swift ad-lib, thinking on your feet to find a solution, but Mike is in it for the long game. He refuses to accept second best in anything.

He is also endlessly appreciative of me. "Eric has a great idea," he will announce to some solution I have whispered to him. He has no need to do this, but there is a precise and generous exactitude in his calling out a credit for something that I have suggested. For example, Casey is against pots on the stage for the explosions. He is rightly concerned that his dancers will slip or catch their feet in them. I suggest we make a pile of bones to conceal them and we bring them on just for that scene. Suggestion taken.

Casey is absolutely dead, beat. Tim Hatley looks exhausted, but his sets are magnificent and even better with Hugh's lighting. Mike, always hovering and pressing, shows me the difference great stagecraft can make to people standing onstage. It's amazing.

THE SITZPROBE

FRIDAY, DECEMBER 17, 2004, 8:00 A.M.

Today is the Sitzprobe. In opera and musical theater, a sitzprobe (from the German for "seated rehearsal") is a rehearsal where the singers sing for the first time with the orchestra, focusing attention on integrating the two groups. But *sitzprobe* sounds so much more exotic. Ours is held in the basement of the Oriental Theatre.

After the despair of Wednesday night, when the first dress rehearsal was an absolute nightmare, when the wardrobe department failed to make a single costume change on time, when we only managed to stagger through act 1 in our allotted four hours, after that evening of disaster that left all the Yanks despondent and all the Brits strangely cheerful, everything has changed. Yesterday the whole company was elated. It was the orchestra that rallied us. The sitzprobe was a love-in. At the end of the two hours, there was a standing ovation. *Elation* is not too strong a word. The songs, heard all together for the first time, kept hitting, each leading into different areas, now funny, now genuinely moving. Larry Hochman's arrangements are fabulous. The whole orchestra plays magnificently under the calm conducting of Todd Ellison. Glen Kelly's careful work has all paid off. Our songs, heard sung by these wonderful people, sound simply great. Suddenly everything is going right. The score is even witty, with now and then big laughs from the company, for the piccolo "Penny Lane" trumpets, for example, or a George Harrison solo, which makes only me sad. "Find Your Grail" had me in tears. Mike says he has never heard a score like it. He compares it with *My Fair Lady* and says that one has duffs and ours doesn't. Wow. Hank said he "would never forget that day." David said it was a wonderful experience. Everyone is filled with happiness and confidence. Our company is so amazing. I sit among the chorus, who are enthusiastic as kids, leaping to their feet to come forward for their numbers. We face the orchestra on metal chairs, there is a line of four microphones around the conductor. The cast moves effortlessly up for their cues, making us laugh with their lead-in dialogue and then killing us with their songs. It all hits, from the silly "Finland" opening, through to the choral ending. We move from the strong powerful voice of Tim and the sweetness of Michael's Patsy through the silliness of Christian (a uniquely gifted clown), to the magnificent control of David, who is cheered to the rafters for his amazingly deft and delicate and hilarious rendition of "You Won't Succeed on Broadway." Add the charm of Hank, the sweetness and confident lunacy of Steve, and top it with the amazing genius of Sara, and it is a heady recipe. I watch the violin ladies staring at Sara open-mouthed as she stretches her voice and blows the room away. The roars of approval at the end of her numbers are genuine. People are in tears and very happy. She emerges as a powerfully strong talent, a new Streisand. The whole basement of the Oriental Theatre is filled with happy, beaming people. We are literally undermining *Mamma Mia!* They are in the theater above. John and I celebrate with oysters and lobster, then an evening of cleanup onstage. Casey has listened to our worries about "Finland" and has changed it. Now everyone will get the gag. It has become an opening filled with energy, confidence, and silliness. Pure Python.

I had a tiny tussle with Mike and the producers because I am serious about playing silly music as the audience enters the theater. I know from long experience that if you play Sousa marches and even Mantovani, the audience loosens up and chatters loudly and feels relaxed. The New Yorkers are horrified when I suggest this. Feeling I am losing the argument I ask the sound department to play "Liberty Bell." Bones, our sound man, puts on the familiar intro.

Dah de-dah de-dah de-dah da diddly dum dee dum. Boing.

At once Mike concedes. They see the instant effect. The whole atmosphere in the theater changes—people are laughing and singing and smiling. It's an extraordinary result. Subliminally of course it's the Python effect, this is after all the theme tune for The Flying Circus, and it whets our appetite for all the nonsense that is to follow, but it is a very enjoyable way to win an argument. So there will be ironic music as they come in. John and I are very happy. After all, we have learned something from touring America!

The wonderful thing about this group of people is that every single one in every area is the best at their game. Everywhere you look there is talent. Onstage this is obvious, but it is just as noticeable (and just as important) off. We are truly blessed. The great thing is that, despite the extraordinary fact we have sold out every seat for our entire run and the extraordinary buzz in Chicago, there is still a grudging reluctance from journalists to embrace this show. This is a good thing. We still have room to surprise them. I don't think they anticipate our score. At the moment they are still making grudging remarks about "not the full Monty," "five of the others not here," etc., etc. But the simple fact is, that for this event, the others would not have helped. They have done everything they needed to do to make it work, including staying out of the way.

MONDAY, DECEMBER 20, 2004, 5:43 A.M.

It's been a roller coaster. But now we're coasting. Tonight is the test. The live dress rehearsal with almost real people. Not entirely real. They are not paying. But tonight we'll learn something about whether it's funny or not.

Each of our two dress rehearsals, filled with unmade costume changes, ended in depression and we were only pulled out of it by the orchestra. When the live band appeared, the cast soared. Now people missing onstage is a thing of the past. The whole show is a smooth-running ship, with just as many people below the waterline as gunners on deck. It's a process, not a miracle. Even the *Times* of London yesterday wished us well in a leader, for heaven's sake. The Brit boys abroad, as I observed to John. This is seen by them as an away match. According to them, we are going to save Broadway. Setting aside the hubris of that, perhaps they are just doing that British one-two, where they set you up and then relish knocking you down. But at least they haven't attacked us off the bat.

Tania and Lily came in yesterday. Lily is determined to avoid everything until the world premiere tomorrow night. And I have prepared a surprise for her. I have put her in Row A, Seat 101, so she will be the first person to have the Grail discovered under her seat and pulled up onstage with the cast. Appropriate, I think. I can't wait to see her face.

I recorded the compulsory precurtain announcements

and was gratified to hear them get huge laughs when they played them back for the cast. The overture sounds wonderful and I spent some time fine-tuning the correct pistol shot in it. Let's hope it's the shot heard round the world.

Tania and I celebrated with a long-awaited *cinq à sept*. I sneaked away as they were rehearsing the curtain calls. The entire cast is in excellent spirits. The producers are looking ecstatic. Bill Haber called this morning and said he didn't know what to say—it had all come together in the few days he was away. It is a process, not a miracle.

Tonight we have some family and tomorrow more and a private party after the show. Heady days. There is pleasant email from Michael Palin and Terry Gilliam, both wishing us good luck. It's nice to feel the Pythons are behind this. Cynthia Cleese is coming tomorrow, too. So it is all very family. I think this may be rather a wonderful thing for our old age. We may have cleverly subverted all the Python reunion demands. John Du Prez wanders around beaming. I feel strangely calm. It's almost like I get before I do a show myself. It'll be interesting to see if I get butterflies. So much is riding on this. Not to mention thirteen million dollars!

DRESS REHEARSAL

TUESDAY, DECEMBER 21, 2004, 6:07 P.M.

Wow. *Spamalot* was a triumph. Its first public dress rehearsal last night opened to prolonged, triumphant laughter. There was delight throughout the auditorium. We grabbed them from the beginning with the glorious silliness of "Finland" and they laughed at the outrageousness of starting the wrong show. They cheered the arrival of Arthur and Patsy. They adored "I Am Not Dead Yet," and Christian throughout was a hit. They simply went nuts for Arthur's cheerleaders, and they laughed themselves silly through "The Song That Goes Like This." "Find Your Grail" was a triumph, "Knights of the Round Table" was sustained hilarity, and they all fell in love with Sara culminating in her French cow cabaret. My concern that "Whatever Happened to My Part?" had no context was no problem at all. They simply laughed at the first line and adored her. She got cheers by the end. It was a showstopper.

The biggest delight and the most surprising was that they simply went nuts for what Mike calls "the Jew song." Mike had been very concerned about this number and he and I were sitting together when David sings:

In any great adventure if you don't want to lose
Victory depends upon the people who you choose.

So listen, Arthur darling, closely to this news,
You won't succeed on Broadway
If you don't have any Jews.

The gale of laughter that greeted this line forced David and the orchestra to wait several moments before he could even start the first verse of the song. And then it was a knockout throughout, from its bottle dance with Grails on their heads to the hilarious conclusion with the descent of the Star of David. The audience cheered long and loudly.

Mike turned to me, smiling in relief. "Well, that's all right, then," he said.

Oddly, the only things that didn't go as well as expected were Python things. The Taunter, greeted by cheers, went on far too long, way past its sell-by date, and I am to look for cuts today. Similarly, the Knights of Ni was too long. There was something a little indulgent in both of these scenes. Mike will fix them. He is itching to cut the opening of act 2 with the Historian and to remove Steve's Mother completely. I begged him to wait twenty-four hours. The cast is in ecstasy and we all expect it to crash tonight with the first paying customers, when it will be easier to make the necessary cuts. Steve Rosen in particular will be hard-hit, as no one liked the Mother in her gold costume at the end. We'll have him come in as Bedevere. The Rabbit drop at the end of act 1 was an anticlimax as I expected, and we have already cut it. They will all stay onstage after "Run Away" (which is to be shortened) and we'll have the curtain fall on them. My only caveat with the numbers was "Bright Side," which the audience sat through with indulgence, rather than any real delight. It doesn't build and, though the umbrellas are nice, they all stop singing to dance.

Some other joys: David's Sir Robin is a triumph, and his little speech about Broadway is wonderful. Said with just the right amount of sincerity.

> *Broadway—is a very special place. Filled with very special people. People who can sing and dance. Often at the same time. People who need people, and who are, in many ways, the luckiest people in the world.*

The Black Knight fight actually worked, and the arms-for-the-poor gag gave us a huge if groaning laugh to cover up Christopher's move back to where he is pinioned and has his legs removed. He was also extremely good as the Father. He is perhaps best as Galahad with his hair in his eyes. He played that to the hilt superbly, tossing his hair affectedly. Prince Herbert was hilarious, largely because Christian is so funny. Tim is great as the mournful, now cheery center of the play as King Arthur, unexpectedly moving us to tears with "I'm All Alone." David was a delight, so tasteful, so touching, and so handsome, while Hank was ecstatic and announced that he wanted to spend the rest of his life in this show!

Afterwards in the lobby, I met the Hormel people, who were very happy, while all our producers were beaming. Bill Haber said he was going to just stay away and we could have as much money as we wanted. Wendy was over the moon with delight. No one has ever experienced reactions like it, and this was only a dress rehearsal! Well, as I said, we all expect it to crash tonight. We are meeting at 12:30 for cuts, and the cast comes in at one for notes. The most urgent thing is to inject some pace into the Witch Village scene that takes an eternity. It drives me nuts, but Mike will fix it, that and the end of act 1, where they will now all stay onstage. But the big surprise and delight, apart from the standing ovation and the cheers which greeted the end of the show, is that we don't have that much to fix. They buy the slender plot, they indulge the Grail found in the audience, and they laugh at the Peasant pulled up onstage. They even like the wedding and Arthur getting Guinevere. I hugged John and kissed Mike. Even the "Bright Side" singalong at the end had them; after a few seconds of uncertainty they got into it, and the surprise cannon and the fall of golden stuff from the ceiling at the end was a delightful touch. Hang the extra cleaning fee! So there it is, a strangely expected and yet somehow unexpected triumph. With the prospect of tonight to see what we have really learned. Certainly the decision to come here was absolutely right, and frankly, bravo us. All that hard work has paid off.

Subj: It's better than CATS!
Date: 12/21/2004, 9:24 a.m., central standard time
From: Mary Alice Buck
To: Eric Idle
Sent from the Internet

Okay, the standing-O probably means more, but I have to
THANK YOU for putting me on the list for last night. What
an absolutely fantastic show—all the great stuff that
everyone loves (and wanted to see) perfectly merged
with so many timely and hilariously funny new jokes—
I have never laughed so hard—EVER—in my life. Cosette
in the French scene just about did me in. And the cast
was having so much fun onstage. Not that you need it
from me, but I predict this show will wipe out any record
The Producers ever thought about making—it's just so
clever and original. What a super fun treat it was to be
there last night—thanks again for including me.

All the best to you, Tania, and Lily for a fantastic
holiday—I think you'll have a great many things to feel
festive about!

Mary Alice

PS—Did you know I was the one who caught the bouquet at
the end? Someone said it means I'm going to marry a Jewish
knight, but I think it just proves my first true love is great
theater!

FIRST PREVIEW

THURSDAY, DECEMBER 23, 2004, 7:37 P.M.

Well, it was no fluke. If we thought the dress went well, then the first preview made it look tame. We killed. Right from the start, they laughed and cheered. Everything that went well before went better; things that didn't go so well now did. Our small tightens and cuts helped. They simply ate up the show. At the end they went nuts and sang along to "Bright Side" at the curtain call and cheered when the gold stuff dropped from the ceiling. We had standing ovations in all three balconies as well as the orchestra. Outside, the lobby was packed and the store broke all merchandise records as we sold over $10,000 worth of stuff!

I sat in Row G, which was great. I could see Lily for the trick I played on her. I sat her in Row A, Seat 101. I could see her starting to understand why, once the Holy Hand Grenade revealed the clue. Lily looked really sweet as Patsy got her to her feet and then insisted she come onstage. Tim was really kind and held her hand and kissed her shoulder and told her softly not to worry as Michael read out the winner for Best Peasant in Chicago.

"And the Arthur goes to Eric Idle's daughter," he said.

Then they all sang her name and she has the Polaroid of the moment with her and the cast plus a little gold Arthur for Best Peasant, the first person ever to win the Arthur and have the Grail discovered beneath them. She had no idea up to that point. Lily was thrilled with her spotlight moment onstage. The cast all loved her and said how lovely she is and no one could believe she is only fourteen.

After the show, when I went forward to collect her and Tania from the front row, there were shouts of my name and suddenly I realized all three balconies had stopped exiting and were all standing and applauding me. I was trapped. So I spread my arms and they cheered, and then I pretended to hide in my jacket. In fact, the audience response was so great, it was hard to get out of the theater with throngs of people refusing to leave and a thousand programs to sign.

Afterwards there was a party at the Atwood, the café in our hotel, and a glorious party it was, too, with everyone happy and relaxed. The Goldstones were beaming, John, who had produced the original movie and all our subsequent movies, with his wife, Linda. Kim Howard Johnson, superfan, was thrilled by the show; Sasha, my beautiful niece, was looking wistfully at Hank; Tania looked glorious and was admired by all the chorus girls; and Lily looked so young and confident and adorable. Thaweesee [Lily's former nanny] was there, too, with Joyce, my sister-in-law, and both Scott and Tracie Hamilton had flown in to experience this first-ever performance. He beamed and smiled and was soon happily surrounded by a crowd of skating fans, surprisingly many amongst our cast.

Last night was the same. A terrific buzz in the theater and

gales of laughter right from the off. Mike brought Diane, and she was looking so beautiful on her birthday. We had spent the night after the first preview going over notes. Mike had a big plan after the dress to push "Find Your Grail" to the position of first act closer, as it gains the greatest response and is the emotional climax of act 1, but after listening to the concerns of Casey and Todd and John, they all encouraged me with my worry that such a move would destroy our plot altogether. The knights must split up at the end of act 1 and be lost in the forest at the start of act 2, leaving Arthur depressed and alone. This sets up everything that happens in act 2. He is quite lost and while searching for his men, he meets the Knights of Ni and the Black Knight and is given the task to find a shrubbery. Eventually he bumps into Robin and they are given another task—to put on a Broadway musical. If Arthur ends act 1 triumphant, we have no story.

I finally spoke up forcefully against this change and Mike said even *he* was now no longer convinced; and at the cast notes after last night's show, he said Casey and I were right, so it looks as though suddenly and amazingly we don't have much to do and have avoided a ton of work next week. We just have to cut the lamer bits, keep the pace moving, and find an end for Bedevere and Patsy. In fact, Mike even announced he was going to leave them all alone for a bit, so clearly he is planning to go home.

We worked on strengthening the "Run Away" bit, and Casey is going to rethink the act 1 finale and work on it next week—we are talking of having the castle revolve and a bit more chaos. But that should do us for the intermission moment.

Re: (no subject)
Date: 12/21/2004, 6:00 p.m., central standard time
From: Mike Nichols
To: Eric Idle

you are the best there ever was and i am so damn lucky.
Xxxxm

Subj: Pythonline draft
Date: 12/22/2004, 2:37 a.m., central standard time
From: Kim Howard Johnson
To: Eric Idle
CC: Adrian Bryan-Brown
Sent from the Internet

Hi, Adrian and Eric,

Here's a little something I drafted for PythOnline—it's 2:30 a.m., so please excuse any typos. I hope it's not too much like a review—I'm just trying to get the fans stirred up and even more excited about the show—but let me know if you want me to change things (or toss it out entirely).

Adrian—very nice meeting you.

Eric—thanks again—it's absolutely wonderful!
All best,

Howard

This is NOT a review—no, more like an aperitif to whet the appetite of starving Python fans. The critics won't get a look at *Spamalot* for nearly three more weeks. No, this is just a word of advice. If you have a chance to nab tickets for *Spamalot* in Chicago between now and Jan. 23, do not hesitate.

I just got back from the very first show, and my brain is hurting from the thunderous ovations the audience delivered throughout the two and a half hours. This is a genuine Broadway spectacular, folks. (As Eric joked, the lawyers' fees for this show are more than the entire budget of the original film.)

The cast is superb. David Hyde Pierce looked as though he were having the time of his life portraying Sir Robin and a few random villagers and guards. Hank Azaria proved to be an inspired casting choice for such Cleese roles as Sir Lancelot, the French Taunter, and Tim the Enchanter. And Tim Curry's King Arthur is the glue that holds the entire company together. I won't single out the rest of the cast, which is superb from top to bottom.

And the songs! Eric and John Du Prez have come up with a smashing array of original songs which, combined with songs featured in the film, make up a delightful score. There's an Andrew Lloyd Webber parody here, a Vegas show there, even a wonderfully witty tweak at *The Producers*. And, yes, the rumors are true—even the cow that is catapulted over the castle wall has a song.

Eric has done the impossible—he's actually come up with the plot that the original *Holy Grail* never quite managed to achieve. Along the way, he fleshes out the characters from the film, creates some new ones, and turns it into a solid piece of theater.

Mike Nichols's staging is nothing short of brilliant, hilarious, and inventive—he knows where the jokes are, and there are plenty of them.

The audience on the first night couldn't get enough of it, gladly giving up a standing ovation and singing along with the cast to "Always Look on the Bright Side of Life" at the close.

If this was a review, I'd go on at great length with even greater enthusiasm, but it's getting late, so I'll sign off for now with these last bits of advice.

Do what you have to do to get tickets to the show in Chicago.

If you can't do that, come to New York, where previews start Feb. 14.

If you can't do either, the soundtrack and other merchandise will soon be available at montypythonsspamalot.com.

MONDAY, JANUARY 3, 2005

The show has been steadily growing and maturing, until now it is a fighting vehicle.

The audience gets with it right from the start and by the end they are standing on their feet screaming. It is undeniably a popular hit with the crowds and the buzz in the city is extraordinary. On our rehearsal days we cut lesser lines, what Mike calls "their babies," treasured moments that they have held on to and which he savagely sweeps away so that the show keeps getting better. Casey has been tightening and shortening the numbers—"Knights of the Round Table," for instance, so that the knights now sing and dance it, which is far more effective. "Rio" has been improved and this week gets another rejig, if poor sick Casey recovers in time. Tania says you can watch it every night, and we do.

"You Won't Succeed on Broadway" has become the time bomb that stops the show. The audience is literally rocked out of their seats. The shock and delight is manifested in waves of noise and applause. When the menorah is placed on the piano, so you get a tiny weird evocation of Liberace, the whole place erupts. Then David plays magnificently and teases the audience until he turns and his whole body shakes into the great Jewish dance. They cannot believe it. They yell and shriek and are happy beyond belief. It is a great wonderful affirmation of Jewishness, and utterly surprising, so that by the end, when Arthur asks, "Are there any Jews here?"

there is a great spontaneous cry of "yes" and even hands go up. This is fabulous. I watch people in the audience at the moment David delivers the first line. They literally come out of their seats. They shriek with laughter, which is followed by an instant moment of anxiety, when they wonder, "Oh my God, which way is this going?" but then a moment later they see in a flash that it is all right. It is the very opposite of a Nazi moment, so that they scream with joy. Something is being said which is very rarely admitted which is both literally true and politically incorrect: *You won't succeed on Broadway if you don't have any Jews.* It came from something Lorne Michaels said to me a long time ago. "We are the leaven that makes the bread rise." I loved that, and somehow my subconscious turned it into that song.

Subj: Sara
Date: 12/22/2004, 2:37 a.m., central standard time
From: Eric Idle
To: Casey Nicholaw
Sent from the Internet

Dear Casey,

Last night we all witnessed something extraordinary. A sight and a power hitherto unsuspected: Sara on the dance floor. At the Nacional 27 nightclub she dominated the circular disco dance floor for four hours. Her stamina, her sex appeal, her sheer erotic dancing blew everyone

away. She is a star in every possible sense. She
shimmied and salsa'd in a tiny fronded Tina Turner dress,
dancing with ease and abandon around and with
everyone. If alone, then by herself; when some of the
boys cornered her, she would dance right back at them.
In the end she gave a sparkling finale with Brad crawling
around on the floor at her feet. It was exciting, unique,
and a total display of bravura superstar power that none
of us has ever seen before and as Mike said at its height,
"This has to go in the show." Even with all our girls at their
finest, even with Abbey boogying away, you could not
take your eyes off Sara. At one point she leaned back
against a pillar and let our boys surround her and pretend
to hump her, then she turned round and putting her
hands on the pillar backed into them. It was dirty dancing
at its most amazing and it would have brought Puerto
Rico to a standstill, let alone Chicago.

We had a brief chat about where this might work and
the natural place is "Rio." She is the Lady of the Lake;
she can affirm Lancelot (du Lac). Her Laker Girls come
on, so it would be entirely appropriate if the beat went
very hot for a break when she could appear in their midst
and shimmy and salsa in a tiny Tina Turner dress.
Lancelot might adopt a series of *Saturday Night Fever*
poses beside her. Later she says to Arthur, "Oh, you
missed that scene," which might as easily refer to this
and works even better when she is present in it. I think

you would need Larry Hochman to write something entirely Latin with a really pulsating percussive salsa beat for a break that could bring the audience to their feet. Think of that great Paul Simon carnival number, "Late in the Evening." The only person who could live with Sara on the dance floor was, wonderfully and magnificently, Tim; and if they both had a fantastic salsa break in the wedding when they come in, the whole ending could go Brazil nuts. We would need to discuss which tune it should be, but this was Mike's idea and it is a very exciting one.

We all missed you and hope you are feeling a bit better.

Eric

Subj: lightning bolt
Date: 1/3/2005, 2:50 a.m., central standard time
From: Mike Nichols
To: Casey Nicholaw

dearest case,

i hope you are feeling a little better. with luck a night's sleep will start you on the road to recovery. i pray. and if you are sick for a while, no better time for it.

the show was great tonight and the party was a revelation. it was a fine place and the food and the dancing were great and all were happy. BUT the real shock was sara. she was gorgeous in a very short disco dress. great legs, ass (forgive me), and whole body. but, case, on the dance floor, she was fucking on fire. rita hayworth would worry. she is a GREAT dancer. you could see no one else on the floor, not abbey, not anyone. we were all totally stunned.

i hate to say it to you but you will have to consider reopening "rio" so we can bring her in with her laker girls and kill with a salsa or something like it. then when she says, "i am as human as you are now," she should be revealed in that hot short dress. then after "twice in every show," they should do a fucking salsa. trust me. tim danced with her and was also amazing. totally manly and flamenco and brilliant. then, when they are into the wedding, with glen's help if we can go into something as hot as that was tonight, presumably with "find your grail," and they can really turn on and dance as they did tonight, people will tear out the seats. i have never seen anything like it. we were all cheering.

i went into this with eric and he wanted it as badly as i do. it is truly exciting and such a shock that it would fit in with our cliché gag and simultaneously be a wild ending, plus showing the two of them in a way we have never seen.

we have not done her a service with her present makeup and even her clothes. she was so shockingly beautiful with her simple makeup and her own hair. we must get with tim and joe and find a way for her to be the beauty that she truly is.

sorry to hit a sick man with so much. obviously it will all wait till you feel okay again. this letter can wait until then, too. i am just so excited that i wanted to start telling you. when you feel right we can begin to discuss all this and take the good amount of time we have after opening here to see if this might all work.

love,

mike

Subj: Re: changes
Date: 1/3/2005, 12:34 p.m., central standard time
From: Mike Nichols
To: Eric Idle

this point about bedevere is excellent and useful. we should start with it when casey comes back from the dead.

we both wrote him very similar letters about last night. i was too drunk with excitement and raw fish to send you a copy so it is now in your inbox.

am very excited. we have to hope we don't kill casey with this news but if anyone is up to it he is. he is the sara of choreographers.

funny that (pointing silently upward, unwilling to piss Him off) has been so good to us. i put it down to the piece of the true cross i got with the help of the CAA guide.

tania was so beautiful last night, in every possible way. but then what else is new?

xxxxm

WEDNESDAY, JANUARY 5, 2005

And so the days pass agreeably. Tania in the next room. Anish Kapoor's Bean (*Cloud Gate*) prominent in my view in Millennium Park. Last night it snowed. The polished metal kidney was etched in snow this morning, against the gray of the lake. After a long meeting in the tiny backstage room, setting goals and targets for what needs to be done and what we can achieve before we leave Chicago, Tania and I cadged a lift with Mike up to Rush Street. It was snowing pleasantly again, the streets picked out in white. Mike wanted to get out and walk the last few yards. We wouldn't let him.

"What if you were to slip, and someone came along and pissed on you," I said, which sent him into paroxysms of laughter. He has been monumental here. He never misses a performance. I have persuaded him not to sit under the shelf downstairs. There you are isolated from the main body of the audience and you cannot hear the laughter bursting from the upper tiers. Tonight at the meeting he points out we will have five hundred less in the Shubert on Broadway, which means the show will go faster, since they won't have to wait for the wave of the laughter to travel all the way to the back and then forward again. The New York Shubert will be more intimate. I hope we made the right choice, since we are packed in this theater. Visiting *All Shook Up* with our cast on Sunday reminded us all of how intimate this theater has become with the genius of Tim Hatley's sets. The clouds above pull us in and the twin castellations on either side lead the eye on to the stage, so that our smallish cast of eighteen makes it seem packed. At their theater, the Cadillac Palace, a much larger cast looked swamped by their stage. Sharon Wilkins is in this, a massive talent, utterly wasted; she was Sour Kangaroo in *Seussical*. And sadly, they miss every important thing about Elvis. How they could select the worst of his music and then make it completely unexciting is almost a talent in itself. It reminds us all how lucky we are. Our cast is more or less unanimously scathing. Mike leaves at the intermission, Hank sighs visibly, David raises a laconic world-weary eyebrow, and Chris brushes past.

"Two block rule," he says.

"What?" Tania and I both say.

"You mustn't talk about what you have just seen within two blocks of leaving a theater. You don't want their relatives and friends hearing devastating remarks."

Of course. It is a kind rule.

We tinkered yesterday with "Rio" and a little bit with Witch Village. We recognize this latter scene as the one that isn't landing. I listened to the song demo again and realized that they go twice as fast, so tonight they slow it down. It really helps, and they are going to cut the screaming. It is way too gruesome to see a young woman being burned and hear her screams, nothing funny about that, and it makes the song heartless. What is funny about the villagers' scene is their jolliness in their pursuit of witches. It makes it at least as understandable as hunting.

We also talk about the transformation scene. Tim has designed a magic dress for Sara, where with one tug of a string her green dress instantly and magically transposes into a wedding dress. This will kill in the penultimate scene. We also want her to be able to rip off the bottom of her wedding dress to reveal a tiny Tina Turner skirt and use her amazing dancer talents.

My relations with the William Morris agency descended even further into opéra bouffe. Johnny Levin, my friend and agent, who has been writing to me and confirming that he is bringing Gary Loveman, the head of Harrah's, to the opening night, finally reveals *He thinks we are in New York*. Oops. Fortunately, Mr. Loveman is part of the private-jet set. He commutes to Vegas from Connecticut anyway and so this only involves a change of route. Johnny is keen to have Gary see the show early, as Johnny quite rightly suspects that Vegas interest will be high. We were already seen by one management, the man who put Queen on, who tells me sadly that the Excalibur Hotel is about to be knocked down.

Mike tells him he wants this show in *every* Vegas hotel. Johnny Levin explains gently that that is unlikely to happen. Our old friend Ben Gannon, who put on the Peter Allen hit for Broadway, writes and asks for the Sydney show. There are several offers for London, including one from my old chum Jim Beach (the Queen manager). Bill Haber responds politely to all of them. He has his own plans. He has to return to NY this week—more than three million dollars are on his desk for the tsunami relief efforts of Save the Children, which he helms.

Casey is back, though still sounding a little thick voiced. He is soon bouncing around on the stage, inspiring people, trying to improvise new dance steps. Eventually he sits down and says, "Ya know what, this is silly. I need to work this out. Let's postpone all this till Thursday."

He is not only bright, intelligent, and inspiring, but very sensible. Mike and I lead him on ever further, encouraging him and exhausting him. But the show sparkles with his genius. The musical numbers land one after another. The audience just loves us by the end. They love the Best Peasant in Chicago coming up and representing them onstage at the end, and they stand happily singing "Always Look on the Bright Side" with the cast at curtain call. They cheer when the confetti bursts loose from above them.

It's snowing again outside my big windows here high on the fifteenth floor. I feel a pleasant tingling feeling. *What is that?* Ah yes. Happiness. It doesn't get much better than this.

A show going well and a beloved wife here on honeymoon. We take tea at the Peninsular, shop, go to movies, have dinner together. Yesterday she slipped into my bed as I was playing guitar and sang a beautiful Beatles song beautifully, even reading the dots. I had never heard her sweet voice. It's one of her favorite songs, she confesses. We harmonize happily together. Sweet and touching.

"Who's going to play you in the movie of us?" I ask her occasionally.

OPENING KNIGHT

MONDAY, JANUARY 10, 2005, 12:35 A.M.

You must feel very proud, they keep telling me. Well, I suppose if I must, I must, but to tell you the truth, I don't know exactly how I feel. I certainly feel proud of our cast. They were magnificent tonight, never withered under fire, never turned a hair. I was excited *before* the show, when I went round, wishing them all well. I told them, and I felt it, genuinely envious of them going out there, but sitting in the audience uncomfortably aware of a battery of critics, sitting far too close and not smiling or responding, I began to be very concerned about the audience. Above and around and in the balconies they were screaming as usual, but all around me they were only smiling. Who were they? These the wealthy, the backers, and the rubbernecking first-nighters.

We hated them. By the intermission Mike and I and the stage manager, Peter Lawrence, all wanted to kill them.

The cast hadn't noticed—the laughs from above and around were rolling in. But we felt an ominous absence in this audience, something we had never yet experienced. Amazingly, immediately after the intermission they were with us. Partly the alcohol, but also I think because they had validated their own reactions about how much fun they were having. Now they loved and applauded "Bright Side," the Knights of Ni brought huge laughs, Sir Robin killed, and then the number that finally rocked the house—the Jew number—that's when they were ours. From then on it was a formality—the charm, the talent, and the sheer ability of our company knocked it out of the park. And yet and yet. I still expect the other shoe to drop. Was it the slightly furtive look on the face of Chris Jones, the theater critic of the *Chicago Trib*, or the fact that one skinny note-taking reviewer scuttled off the minute the curtain fell? I don't trust them. Fuck it, but I don't.

The after-party was filled with happy laughing Jews and gentiles. Held in the lobby of the LaSalle Bank, with knightly decor, the investors looked pleased, and were not shy to come up and say so. One, an Illinois state senator, married to Hugh Hefner's daughter, kept giving me a line from the Passover Haggadah: "What makes this night different from all other nights?"

Turns out he was not only drunk but a very ex-senator.

Michael Gorfaine and Sam Schwartz, the music talent agents, were genuinely bowled over: "Groundbreaking and original and utterly wonderful. It makes other musicals redundant."

Everyone said it exceeded their expectations. Johnny Levin loved it. Ellen Hoberman, my lawyer Tom's lovely wife, was the most fulsome. The party became fun once people cleared out and our company took to the dance floor en masse. A nice Caribbean jump-up brought them out in force. Sara, of course, with her raven hair in a revealing black dress led the way. Fun for me to dance with Lily and Tania. So all ended well, but these events as life are overrated. There is too much other stuff around, too much at stake to be fun. . . .

Good to see Kim Howard Johnson and Hans ten Cate, the Python fan who ran The Daily Lama, and now PythOnline, both brimming with enthusiasm. I never saw Mike. I guess he scuttled early. Too bad, he would have loved all our chorus dancing at the end. Boy, they are something. Such a great group of people. They are all planning to go to some drag club later, but Lily is tired and underage anyway, so we came home. . . .

I guess I'll know in a day or two, but right now I honestly don't know how I feel.

WEDNESDAY, JANUARY 19, 2005, 6:50 A.M.

Mike Nichols is an utter total genius. His work over the last six days has been little short of remarkable. His main strength is a relentless refusal to give up on even the tiniest detail. His script surgery, which is deft and severe at the same time, always saves the life of the patient.

We were in great shape. Our reviews were great, apparently. I stuck to my guns and didn't read them. One or two apparently grudging, one or two resentful and picky, but all saying it's a hit and many outright raves. Including one from Michael Riedel—an apparently vicious critic in the *New York Post* whom everyone hates and fears. But he talked to me the next day on the phone, filled with enthusiasm, and apparently gave us a rave which resulted in—wait for it— $350,000 worth of sales next day at the box office in New York! We are now over ten million dollars advance, halfway to Bill Haber's dream total of twenty million before we open, with still a month to go. This is major box office.

We could have been content to rest on our laurels and slide into NY on the great word of mouth it is generating. (It really does make people happy.) But not Mike. Oh no. First of all he cuts his favorite number: the "Cow Song." The song he adores. He suggests it to me and I have to say it makes sense. It isn't landing. It *is* a tour de force, but it has unwittingly become a slight steal from Madeline Kahn in *Blazing Saddles*. It is a camp cabaret number, it lowers the mood of hysteria built up by "Find Your Grail," and it takes us into the intermission with the admittedly second-rate "Run Away" on not the greatest high point. We get 'em back in act 2, but Mike's surgery is savage. He breaks it to the brave and brilliant Sara, who of course says whatever is good for the show through her tears of disappointment, then asks for the dress and a place on the CD. Smart, brilliant, amazing lady that she is.

People are shocked, there is even rebellion in the camp— people backstage go around muttering. John even raises a revolt, but we say pragmatically and unarguably, "Let's see it without." I am sick as a dog for the rehearsal in which he cuts it, but fortunately the day before I sent in a pile of suggestions for the French scene that will replace it. They will all enter now as French clichés to admire "the art" of the Wooden Rabbit. Then the stuffed cow will be thrown, squashing Patsy, and we will run away into the intermission. Peter Lawrence also argues against the Cow cut—he loves the scene, the mood, the costumes, the French, the Sara— but then, like the pro he is, he takes Mike's arguments. I have no problem with the suggestion. Something instinctively tells me Mike is right. If we can get to the intermission with them buzzing, then I will be a happy man. We will see how it plays.

I eventually recover from my night of horror—food poisoning, a double whammy, sitting on the toilet throwing up at both ends. Yuck. I feel like death, but stay in bed all

Thursday and Mike picks me up and flies me with him on an old G2 (with Diane) to LA, he for the Globes, me for a relaxing weekend with my wife and daughter.

I wrestle with the next problem, Witch Village, which Mike feels isn't landing. Part of the problem is that Hank and David are playing different characters to Lancelot and Robin, which in this context simply doesn't work. There are various theories, but half the audience think they are the same people, the whole burning-a-witch thing isn't landing, and neither is the number. It's partly the fault of the song, but Steve Rosen doesn't sell it particularly well, and sadly it isn't funny. I try several things and eventually take David and Hank out as the village idiots and put them in as Robin and Lance on their way to war overtaken by these blood-thirsty idiots. This has the advantage of allowing us to know who they are and they can see Arthur and they can join in the song so that at least three of the most-talented guys are beside Steve, which strengthens the number when they re-hearse it. So rehearse it we do all through Tuesday after-noon, and Mike is still not happy and finally with ten minutes to go he suggests cutting the whole scene. It's some-thing he has wanted to do and he wants to try it and this is our last chance to see what it is like without it, etc.

He is told, yes, it will be possible, but only if Steve is taken out of being Mother at the end and his couple of lines given to Patsy, which is what we do, and by the skin of our teeth try it once before the stage goes dark. So there is much excitement for tonight. Will they make these trims? Of course, poor Steve is immediately unhappy. He is very young and this is his first big musical and he has just lost his only song.

I bet Mike we will be very short in act 1.

"We'll still be over an hour," he says and I instantly produce cash. Luckily for him only five dollars. I know we will be under an hour, we haven't been over an hour in act 1 in weeks. . . .

The show is a triumph. Act 1 flies by. The thing goes so well it's a few moments before I realize we have gone past the Witch Scene without even noticing the omission. After "The Song That Goes Like This," Arthur recruits Galahad, the Historian comes in, and we see the rest of the knights he has rounded up. The plot is so simple and so straightforward that there is now no possibility that the Witch Scene will return. And as for the Cow, well, the French scene gets huge laughs, Patsy being squashed gets huge laughs, and we are into the intermission with a happy and exhilarated crowd. No question it works. Casey and I are utterly excited. We twitter together, and the beam of joy in his intelligent and simpatico eyes is unmistakable. We are both delirious.

"Oh my God," we say.

The act has come in at forty-four minutes! Haber is brooding and brings up the Cow and mutters something about how it has all become a sketch show.

"*Monty Python is* a sketch show," I say unsympathetically. His case has no hope. Mike, too, is excited. We all cluster outside Tim's dressing room. He started so well and so brilliantly then took a terrible tumble in Camelot, falling backwards over the outsize dice onto his bad back, losing his crown and appearing momentarily dazed and shaken, but he found himself, people picked him up, and he went straight on with the number. Sara never even noticed.

Act 2 goes even better than usual. The audience is right with it—they cannot wait for the curtain to open—and the calls at the end are a riot. I feel very sorry for him, but Steve takes his call resentfully and lurks at the side of the stage like a sardonic Iago. They still cheer Sara. She has lost the Witch and the Cow, but she is still brilliant in all her numbers, and oddly we have got back to the part which I wrote for her: the Lady of the Lake. The parts she has lost are the extra bits that were given to her because we couldn't find a Zoot.

Backstage in the airless room there is a brooding silence from John and Bill. I sense a simmering rebellion. But they have no chance with Mike, me, and Casey all elated and united, what hope do they have? I know it's none. Mike is a little late and comes in, furious. Steve Rosen has demanded that "he must have a scene written to introduce his Bedevere character."

A first-timer, and a very lucky boy, lecturing Mike.

"How long shall I give him?" Mike asks.

"Five minutes," I suggest.

"Tell him right now," says Casey; and out from him and Peter come a litany of complaints.

Mike offers to fire him.

My God, he's quick.

Peter says there is no need for that but Mike must speak to him.

"This is the crossroads for him," says Mike. "He either takes it and understands or he becomes an asshole."

Mike will talk to him tomorrow and show him how he is behaving badly. Steve has lost the sympathy of everyone and even though he has the saintly Michael McGrath with him, he is not listening to the wisdom of Michael, who has seen it all and been through it all and remains smiling and, after having nothing very much going in, has emerged as a total delight, singing "Bright Side" and making "All Alone" a big success. Steve, on the other hand, had a huge part that I wrote for Jim Piddock entirely pruned and bit by bit ripped away. It is partly the part and partly because he isn't yet good enough. Easy to say, hard to live with, but he is lucky to be in this company. So Steve will face his Waterloo today. He had better watch it. I can see Mike itching to fire him. He asks Haber if there are serious financial consequences. We are probably still paying off Doug. . . . *

––––––––––

––––––––––

* Luckily Steve learns from Mike and becomes an important and supportive member of the company. He is now a staunch and hilarious Broadway producer, writer, and comedian.

So we go through the things we can fix. Mike still wants some work on Arthur's speech. He is relentless. I take notes as he throws out suggestions. Single words but somehow painting exactly what is missing from the scene. He knows I'll produce something from this. I don't have to say anything. We now have such a shorthand, such a complicity, he knows he can trust me and he knows I utterly trust him. I have just shown him my faith. Hasn't he just cut the Cow and the Witch and haven't I just told him he is a genius for doing that? I think the weekend in LA recharged both our batteries. Our wives, the springtime weather, the different change of life, and we see the show fresh. It is clear. We are close.

But there is still the elephant in the room. Bill leaves it to John to make the plea for the Cow, but I can tell that even John knows it is hopeless. He has written a long email at the weekend which I didn't read, because, as I told him, I wanted to see the cowless show first, *without prejudice* as the lawyers say. If it works without, then the case to restore it is very weak. Not only does the play now work, it works for all the reasons Mike now very patiently repeats for John's benefit. It is a scene with very limited appeal, only for the few, the majority of the audience are totally puzzled by it, and it doesn't pay off when this glorious woman is suddenly transmuted into a badly stuffed cow. The audience is mystified and we lose them. Secondly, and I suspect most importantly for Mike, we have unfortunately strayed into Madeline Kahn's territory in the Mel Brooks classic *Blazing Saddles*, and this is not good news at all. John doesn't get very far with his rebellion. Mike is icily clear. There is to be no going back. Casey and I are thrilled. But the meeting is over.

I go home elated.

Outside there is a blizzard, and there is already snow on the ground. We dash for the car in the freezing horizontal snow. In the car I thank Mike for his brilliant surgery.

"Well, he is amongst the top seven hundred film directors, you know," Bill says sardonically.

He knows he has lost. But that is why we have Mike. Is there anyone else who could have wielded the knife so swiftly and so effectively? We now have a show with almost no weak patches at all.

"I think we just added two years to the run," he said in the dressing room. "Once the people from New Jersey get there and then Pennsylvania . . ." he says, his voice trailing off into hopelessness.

"Much sooner than you think," adds Peter, the experienced pro. What an Enobarbus he is. He supports Mike utterly. Who else could have made those instant changes that allowed us to drop the witch scene and make the change flawlessly in less than ten minutes? It was a masterwork. We have geniuses in every department.

Back at the hotel I finally read John's email. We have achieved victory. It is important to heal.

Subj: Cutting the Cow
Date: 1/16/2005, 6:43 p.m., central standard time
From: John Du Prez
To: Eric Idle, Mike Nichols, Casey Nicholaw, and Bill Haber

Dearest Colleagues,

I think the question of cutting the "Cow Song" boils down to head v. heart, intellect v. emotion, book v. score.

I've seen the cut version twice now and while conceding that it works, I can't escape the sense of loss. I would prefer a dramatic excuse to keep it rather than a dramatic reason to cut it. Given the choice to like it or lump it, I will opt for lump it. I think the "Cow Song," a very fine piece, has been sacrificed to justify "Run Away," a very mediocre/poor piece. Musically, I could forgive "Run Away" as a sort of postscript to "Cow," which sent the audience into the lobby very happy for the interval (having spent so much time in the lobby eavesdropping on conversations, the (very positive) talk was always of the Cow number as it was so fresh in their minds). On its own it is a very weak musical ending to act 1.

I could and will sum up the latest effort as "polishing a turd." In short, we have thrown away a musical gem in return for what the Bible calls a mess of potage.

Here's some things I don't like:

(1) The cut seems in part to be a reaction to the tittle-tattle of the press reptiles. I have nothing but contempt

for them. They are riddled with inaccuracies. To say that we ripped this off from *Blazing Saddles* is a cheap lie. To take note of them is to let them win. I have no high moral ground here. I want the show to be a huge commercial success. But my litmus is the ticket-buying public, not the myopic press. The former loved it—I was there. Some of the latter hated it—I don't care.

(2) The cast, God bless 'em, have taken this cut with much fortitude and professionalism. Sara primus inter pares. But the feeling seems to be, "If the leg must be amputated to save the body, so be it." I think that is not a correct analysis. Many have said to me they want the song reprieved. I think we should try to find a creative solution. The most extreme opinion took me aback. . . .

"They have robbed Sara of her Tony."

(3) By wheeling in the "French People" to view the Rabbit, the production values of the costumes are way over the top. Had we not had them lying around, we would never have done it. We seem to be saying, "They are French. They are inherently funny." I think we can leave that stuff to Bush. The man in front of me at this afternoon's performance said, "I didn't like the French stuff, it's way too offensive." Sure, it's anecdotal and he was probably Canadian. So let's lose no sleep. However, we laugh at the Taunter, but he does have the upper hand.

(4) As Mike said, our unique quality is "Moving and Funny at the Same Time." By removing the "Cow Song" we remove a prime example and leave untouched many areas which do not qualify.

Okay, I'll shut up now.

JDP

PS: Musicals are about good songs. (Shum mistake here? Ed.)

I close my computer. I'll reply tomorrow. What I want to say I'll probably never send. I scribble it down on a piece of paper, knowing I'll not send it.

It is interesting to me that when people raise head v. heart, they always assume that thinking with your heart is somehow morally superior to using your brain. Well, bollocks. You might as well talk about farting with your elbow. Your head is what does the thinking for you to spare you from the emotional mess you get into when you let your emotions lead. My head tells me the show is much better for the cuts and my heart is sorry for those who disagree and for Sara, but that's it. The thinking-with-your-heart bullshit is Disney-executive think. It is dangerously sentimental balls. Your heart is an organ that pumps blood. It is snobbery to think you can think better with a pump than the amazing brain we have evolved.

I am pleased with this thought and tinkered with making it into a song, and then I consider using it as the basis for my NY YMCA speech. It has hovered in my notebooks for some time as a potential anti-Disney song.

Subj: RE: Cutting the Cow
Date: 1/17/2005, 11:14 a.m., central standard time
From: Casey Nicholaw
To: Mike Nichols, Eric Idle, John Du Prez, Bill Haber

Hi, everyone! I agree with many of John's points. And I will back any decision that is made. I do want to add a few things, though.

I agree that it does work without the song, and I don't miss it in the arc of act 1—though I did love it, and loved it in the show. I have heard many different comments from people who've seen the show—from "it's so funny and clever" to it's a "big yawn moment." So I don't think we can listen to everything we hear. I agree it is a head vs. heart thing, but I think, more importantly, we now have to listen to our "gut" more than the other two. This is the juncture in the process of an original musical where I have seen a few of them fall apart because too many opinions were listened to, and too many people were trying to be pleased. And I've heard all of us say that recently, so I think our constant reminding each other of that would be a good thing. The bottom line seems to be we should make decisions based on what is right for the show, moment, storytelling, pace, rather than what we are attached to, or what we're hearing other people say.

As far as cast members wanting us to put it back in—I've also heard from many that don't. And being a former actor—they are not a good judge at this point because they are not watching—they are only trying to hold on to moments that feel good for them to do. I've been shocked as an actor when I've stepped out to watch a show at some of the things that worked and didn't, because you really don't have a true sense up there. And I have to say the comment about "they" (meaning "us") robbing Sara of a Tony actually angers me. No one is robbing Sara of anything, and God knows it's the last thing any of us would want to do. But I do feel act 1 was a little off balance as the "Sara show." I had two friends come see two different shows since the song was cut, and they both LOVED her, and one actually said, "Well, they should just hand her the Tony NOW." So that actually made me breathe easier.

All of that said, I would honestly be happy either way. You've heard reactions from John and me, and I look forward to all of you seeing it and weighing in with a fresh eye, especially now that it has played this way for a few performances.

Till Tuesday . . .

Love, Casey

Subj: Bravo, Maestro
Date: 1/19/2005
From: Eric Idle
To: Mike Nichols

Mike, I cannot let the day go too far without
congratulating you on your brilliant surgery. You have
the finest instincts and you listen to them and act on
them with the consummate skill of the great comedian
who sits in your soul. Bravo. I am elated.

I think what you did yesterday was genius. I think
your script surgery on the Cow—cutting your own "baby"
was brilliant—seeing it all come together fresh and clean
and with nothing to sit through and hope it would pass
was a revelation. You have done it. It is a triumph. It is
absolutely unstoppable. Thank you, thank you, and for
your eloquent squishing of the potential post show
emotional rebellion. Casey and I were overjoyed.

But you still owe me five bucks. . . . And, yes, I will
work on Arthur, and see where I get.

It has been a joy and a delight working on this with
you. A discovery, a revelation, and the thrill of a lifetime.
My God, we did it! Can we share five minutes of joy
before our cynical selves curl back like protective
carapaces. Are we really snails?

Eh bien. What joy, what rapture. Let me know if you
need me for emotional support with Steve or afterwards.

I was thinking of going to the Art Institute and then the evening performance—does that seem so terribly wrong?

I love you madly and even more if that is possible.

Yr grateful scribe and pal,

E

Subj: Re: Bravo, Maestro
Date: 1/19/2005, 8:58 a.m., central standard time
From: Mike Nichols
To: Eric Idle

well, my turn to cry. i did so because i love you so much and you are a miracle of unsentimentality and making work the best it possibly can be. that is a full half of life while the other half, the love part and the family it engenders, are your other masterpiece. in other words you have brought happiness to many, created a great human in lily, and now changed the lives of all of us connected, and that is the word, all right, with the show. that is a successful life, my dear friend.

i won't forget the words you wrote me and i won't stop thanking you and Whatshisname, The One Who Has Been Out to Lunch, for this connection with the last show of my life, and the best.

always,

xxxxm

MONDAY, JANUARY 24, 2005

So it was all a dream . . . I'm home. After being delayed
twenty-four hours I finally made it out on a plane that was
early! On a sunny Sunday Chicago morning we lifted out of
the freezing white plains and headed west. Nothing is heading east, New York and Boston are both shut down by the
blizzard that finally left us. Driving through the five-foot
banks of snow on the way to the airport I even felt sad to be
leaving Chicago. It has been very kind to us. As Mike said,
we have achieved everything and more here than we could
possibly expect. He sensibly got out on Friday, but I stayed
for a book signing in our shop (over $2K of biz on my book
The Greedy Bastard Diary), a photo shoot for *Men's Health*,
and the publicity shoot for the cast. This was the most fun,
as the cast sat around in the orchestra in costume gently
bantering, ribbing, and encouraging each other. They are
the most affectionate team; they support and admire and
love one another. It is a joy to be part of them. I'm there to
keep an eye on things we might need for the souvenir bro-
chure, a self-elected role but one that has dragged out a ton
of ideas that I have scrawled in three color Sharpies inside a
cheap plastic file. You just can't keep a silly book writer
down. We'll have this thing out by April and the current
plan is to include one of our demos, an outtake, probably
what we used to call the Lady of the Lake, but will now call

Soggy Old Blondes. The Friday show was hot and hilarious and it was supposed to be my farewell to the show, but by the time we left the theater there was a blizzard and four inches of snow—cars were gingerly fishtailing down the street at five miles an hour. I asked Sara, John Du Prez, Tim, and Mike McGrath to dinner and we barreled into the cars, but, man, it was blowing and cold. A warm restaurant later and the astute and adorable Sara snuck off and paid for us all. Gibsons is fun and packed and has only one flaw when they proudly bring out huge marble slabs of meat to show off their cuts . . . yuck. I haven't eaten meat for almost thirty years. In the car ride on the way home Sara confides an interest in opening the show in London (and Sydney) if she doesn't have to stay forever. Smart lady.

On the way into the hotel my flight for the next day was already showing canceled, so I canceled my car—I knew I was going nowhere Saturday. Best see the show again. Which I did (twice); and to give myself a little fillip, I suggested to Christian that I come on as the Historian at the start of act 2, then he could come on and tell me to "fuck off." He liked that idea. Peter, the stage manager, was nuts about it, so I dressed up in the second costume, with the Historian's tweed jacket and waistcoat and bow tie, and stepped out onto the stage. Most of the cast was in the wings. I wasn't sure what the reaction would be, but I could never have expected how it was: the audience went absolutely crazy, there was a roar and then applause and then cheering and then a standing ovation. They wouldn't stop. I didn't know what to do. I tried to deadpan my way through and hope they'd stop so I could say my one line. But they wouldn't. In the end I had to smile and nod and recognize them, and even then they wouldn't stop; so I gestured for about a minute for them to quieten. Only then could I say my line. Then there was Christian standing next to me with hands on hips. "Fuck off, Idle," he said and I exited meekly to roars of laughter. "Everyone wants to be a comedian," he ad-libbed. . . . But it sure started act 2 with a wallop and the cast were overjoyed. "Thanks for waking them up," said Tim and David.

I return to a hot LA. No one is home but the dog pack, who greet me joyously. I sit in the warm sun and eventually the pink house fills with females, Tania, Lily, her friend Katy, and her Fairy Godmother Lauren Hutton. Lily and I swim and then jump in the Jacuzzi. All that cold forgotten.

Daily Performance Report	
The Shubert Theatre	**Date: Sat. Eve., January 22, 2005**
Chicago	**Performance 16 (+ 22 Previews)**

	Up	Down	Time	Calling SM	Mahlon Kruse
Act 1	8:04	8:54	49:36	Deck	Woolley/Wolff
Intermission			20	Mix	Bones
Act 2	9:14	10:14	59:36	Weather	Lotsa Snow
Playing Time			1:49	Observing	Peter/Darlene
Running Time			2:10	Standing Ov.	Is the Pope Polish??

IN/OUT

OUT	ON	ROLE	REASON
Ariel Reid	Pam Remler	Ensemble	Illness

LATE:

Hank Azaria 11 minutes late for $1/2$ Hr. No Call

ACCIDENT REPORT:
David Pierce stabbed by Lancelot in the Guards Scene. David is not hurt in any way, he has many layers of fabric between him and the wooden sword.

NOTES:

At the top of act 2, Eric Idle appeared as a Faux Historian in his own costume. He began the Historian's speech to loud cheers and applause from the audience, and was then interrupted (planned) by Christian, who said, "Fuck off, Idle." Eric promptly, obediently, left the stage—again to great cheers.

Two great shows from our Pam Remler today. Hoping to have Ariel back tomorrow.

The snow has prevented Gene O'Donovan from coming to Chicago—he'll stay in NYC to begin the load-in. Mike Martinez could not fly out today as planned and will try again tomorrow. The snow seems to have finally ended.

Subj: Re: (no subject)
Date: 1/22/2005, 3:23 p.m., central standard time
From: Mike Nichols
To: Eric Idle

am reading on in your book now that i am in front of the fire with my beloved wife and dog. your childhood is something that i can't get out of my head. we are so inoculated against our own. it is like a memory of some dickens classic comic and has no feeling attached. yours moves me a lot. maybe we can get drunk and laugh about them both someday but we have better reasons to get drunk together. or even better, not.

Date: 1/25/2005, 4.54 a.m. Pacific time
From: Eric Idle
To: Mike Nichols

I was struck by something you said in your last email.

I find memories come rising up like methane bubbles from the hidden lurking depths of my subconscious, sometimes in the form of dreams, daydreams, unbidden reveries. I find more and more as I get older I can access a past that I had forgotten about. But the question what relation does it play to our current self is interesting. Is that boy me? Not anymore, but his anxieties and fears, his habits of being, they carry over surely?

I woke up dreaming of Studley. Something to do with how we work as bionic mechanisms. Is it because I have been thinking about memory that memories rise unbidden?

My mind created a bridge into memory. My dream was of returning to this town now utterly changed, and seeking familiar sights, names, and places inside it.

I loved my mum. Something in my anger and frustration with her I was repressing. She would have loved *Spamalot*.

PART VI

—

The New York
Opening

Ten days to go till the opening of *Spamalot* and I'm back in my little Broadway hotel room after the worst week of my life. This is the worst thing that has ever happened to me. Worse than the death of my mother, worse than the death of my dear friend. If ever there was a perspective to view "success" on Broadway, this is it. To see your little girl turn into Ophelia is desperately sad. To watch a daughter you love, beyond the power to express, become some other person, to hear her talk and behave like a different individual, to see her still look the same, but acting manically with crazy determination, urgently undertaking endless tasks of sorting and cleaning, writing lists, shopping, organizing for some new life ahead that only she can see, this is utterly saddening.

It has become clear that Lily has been poisoned by Zoloft that has triggered a severe bipolar episode. We all react in different degrees of uselessness, with helpless tears, with angry frustration, with hopeless despair.

Barbara, my shrink, is helpful: "At these times it is all too easy to bring out the worst in each of you."

How true. We don't know what to do. *What happened?* Where did this come from? Are we to blame? Tania is weary with helplessness. She repeats, "I don't know what to do" constantly, as if this powerlessness is itself some kind of affront. Which is how it feels.

I, of course, feel responsible. I have been absent these many months, fathering a musical. What a terrible price to pay for success. But then isn't success always at some terrible price?

Fortunately there are signs that my daughter's sickness may be temporary. I am urged by doctors and counselors to continue my week as planned and I head off with a heavy heart for Broadway.

SATURDAY, MARCH 12, 2005, 7:05 P.M.

Now that Lily is through the valley of the shadow and seems, by all accounts, to be returning to her lovely self, even attending school and going to parties, I can begin my ascent of the walls of the canyon of depression that have cast a dark shadow over me, removing all the joy from my life and draining the undoubted pleasure that I must now try and enjoy in the fast-becoming phenomenon that is *Spamalot*. In New York City it is everywhere. I draw up alongside buses with their sides bannered in *Spamalot*. The name *Monty Python* mocks me from the interior of cabs, as I wonder what I am doing here.

What I am doing here is television. And radio. And newspapers. I have essentially become a walking billboard. I am interviewed on morning TV shows and, since they expect it, I do my best to cut loose. On the *Tony Danza Show*, I find myself leaning back and putting my feet up on the leather pouf and then letting my bottom slide off the chair so that I am soon sitting on the floor with my legs in the air, and Tony has the nous to join me down there. We do the interview from the floor.

At the end I pick up my guitar and sing "Always Look on the Bright Side," swapping verses with Tony. I look into the camera to find the lyrics scrolling there and it so throws me I wander disconcertingly off text, which panics Tony, but we segue nicely into another chorus. No one would ever notice.

"Life's a piece of spit?"

Whatever. The whole audience joins in enthusiastically. Tony glows with happiness.

THE FINAL WEEK

MONDAY, MARCH 14, 2005

This process has been the most benign and happily creative time of my entire life. Where are the bitchy screaming fits, the knives in the back, the desperate calls to the lawyers?

The Broadway lawyer Marsha Brooks warned me that the process would be bloody and unpleasant. She didn't say that that would be simply dealing with her. Perhaps the best thing I did was to persuade the Pythons to ignore what she had carefully negotiated—that we might not use the name *Monty Python* above the title. Not permitting it always seemed like madness to me.

"Do you really want to walk down Broadway and see *Spamalot* in lights and not the name *Monty Python*?" I asked when I went back to confirm that that is really what they wanted.

Thankfully they finally saw the force of this argument. The branding of our name alone is worth a ton of money to them. And if the show is a hit, *Spamalot* will lift all boats.

This morning we pretaped the *Today* show for later in the week. Me, Tim, Hank, and David with Katie Couric. NBC has prepared a set, with four medieval suits of armor, a round table, and places set with a Spam salad. I kid you not. Some mad art director has carved medieval towers of Spam and cut out more letters in Spam to spell out the word *Spamalot*. The whole studio reeks of Spam, which is, forgive me, offal.

We are delayed taping because of a breaking story of an Atlanta rapist escaping from a courtroom after shooting at the judge and several others with a deputy's gun. Luckily no one is killed. While we await Katie, we concoct a funny start for the interview. Soon, they are done with the breaking news and we can begin taping.

Katie comes in and settles and asks the first question, upon which we all begin speaking at once. We do not stop. It brings howls of glee from the crew and the people crowded into the studio to see us all. Patiently, she starts again. We all talk at once again. Finally she says, "Hank" severely, and asks him a question meant just for him. In unspoken agreement Tim, David, and I immediately answer for him. Huge crew laughs. They haven't seen this sort of misbehavior since Robin Williams was last here.

Somehow Katie manages to steer us back towards a fairly sensible interview, but we are very subversive; and I totally refuse to answer any serious question, claiming that Monty Python started in 1342 in the Augsburg Empire, wherever the hell that might be. At the end I pick up my guitar and we all sing "Always Look on the Bright Side of Life."

This will air on Thursday, the opening morning of *Spamalot*. Bill Haber is ecstatic in an email and expects us to have a huge bump in the box office. Not that it is slow. We stand at a $16 million advance with slightly less than three days to go. But the nightly preview audience in the Shubert Theatre is adamant that this is a hit. They are going apeshit. And the maître d's know, in the way that they know everything.

One tells me, "This is going to be bigger than *The Producers*."

So, yes, the buzz is great, and the friends who come by have admiration in their eyes and only breathless praise. People come backstage beaming. Today I was greeted and grabbed and praised by the amazing Frances McDormand and the adorable Edie Falco (Mrs. Soprano). She had apparently gone to the sound booth before the show and asked if I was in it.

After the show—when Robin and Marsha Williams came and David Schwimmer said hello backstage and Barry Diller was all aglow with praise—at dinner that night Mike told stories of Jackie Onassis. Sara Ramirez listened with wide eyes. She cannot believe she is hearing this. There is a joy and a delight in watching her join what Mike calls the high table. She knows what is in store for her as a train of men come and gush at her. She is truly a magnificent talent, and gives me a lift home in her waiting limo, a new delight for her; she is impressed and thrilled that she has a black Mercedes waiting.

I have already announced on TV that I have slept with everyone in the cast, including all the boys. Jon Stewart's eyes gleamed with joy.

Everywhere one turns there are magazine interviews and photographs of *Spamalot*. In one article it says that John Cleese has magnanimously lent his apartment to Tim. I mention it to Tim and he lifts a lugubrious eyebrow.

"Yes, at twenty thousand a month."

Very magnanimous.

Mike Palin called me yesterday from the Peninsular in LA, where he is clearly feeling the heat of *Spamalot*. He is effusive and congratulatory and very nice. I tell him he is going to have the delight of hearing the audience screaming with laughter at his writing. Which is true.

Maybe this thing will pass off okay.

The whole experience has been remarkable; and most of the credit for this must go to two early, vital decisions: first of all Bill Haber as producer, and second Mike Nichols as director. *Mike's* most important decision was picking Casey Nicholaw to choreograph. It is Casey's genius and enthusiasm and above all the force of aggressive kindliness in his character that has carried the whole cast through this long journey. His boundless energy, his willingness to go the last mile, to listen to what is being offered, his refusal to put up with dross, and his reluctance to ever finish a number once he has got it working splendidly. This extra effort is what you do on your first show, and I think the same could be said of me, whose rewriting resources were plumbed and exploited to the full in the six weeks of New York rehearsal.

Now I face the opening with trepidation, because there have been many sacrifices for me, not the least holed up in a New York hotel room for months with the subsequent effect on wife and daughter. I of course want to run away right now. I'm not lying when I say it is the process that enthralls me, not the success, which is not success at all but hype and bullshit. But I must go through with it, because that's the job.

Michael Viner a long time ago accused me of not having the character for success, and I think at the time he was right. It was an accurate criticism. It's an English thing to prefer failure, and to somehow associate it with good character. Now I have to see if I have matured enough to go through the blinding eye of the forthcoming storm maintaining some dignity, some friends, and all lovers. For it is my marriage that is most threatened by these long absences. Being alone and frustrated has left me resentful and in need of attention and spoiling. I have forgotten what happiness is, but, as I am a good boarding school boy, I can grind through the weeks dutifully. Now somehow I have to find the character to face with dignity the people praising me, instead of the fear of having it all snatched away. This deep down abiding pessimism, this fear of ultimate abandonment must be the closest experience to being me. Time to no longer trust it. Not to *expect* success but also not to cling to the anticipation of disappointment. I simply must avoid the British vice of snatching defeat from the jaws of victory. That is after all why I left Britain, and if I haven't entirely become American, I have certainly abandoned all that British negativity for a newer and more optimistic life of possibilities on this side of the pond.

OPENING KNIGHT

ST. PATRICK'S DAY, THURSDAY, MARCH 17, 2005

Mountains of opening-night gifts flood into my room overlooking 44th Street. In the afternoon Luke, my hairdresser, comes in to dress my hair. We giggle and talk as he fixes it in the hotel bathroom. Every other room on the floor has someone in our family getting ready, Tania, Lily, Lily's former nanny Thaweesee, our niece Sasha, our friend Tamar, and Joyce, my sister-in-law. Luke will do them all.

"It's like a wedding," he says.

Resplendent in my new charcoal cashmere coat, a delightful and thoughtful present from Bill Haber because it is really chilly out there, I walk to the theater from the back entrance of my hotel down 45th Street and across Times Square. I am thinking to myself, as I am walking to my first Broadway opening, I must remember this and how it feels.

I am elegant in a new Issey Miyake tux with a white shirt and an outrageous Day-Glo collar and what looks like a tie in luminescent green. Smart but silly. I am aware that the picture we are about to take of the remaining five Pythons will not only go round the world, it will be the one used of us for the next ten years, or forever if we never meet again. It's seven years since our last picture together, taken at the Aspen Comedy Festival in 1998. Python fame only seems to get bigger.

Shubert Alley is closed off with security people who recognize me and let me through. Backstage is filled with happy laughing people from *Fiddler on the Roof.* Harvey Fierstein leads in a crowd of actors for the Gypsy Robe presentation on the stage of the Shubert, which Harvey in his wonderful precise voice outlines to me.

"Many years ago in the fifties," he says, "there was a chorus girl who was very nervous, and to calm her nerves her leading man gave her a robe which he said had been worn by all the leading chorus girls on Broadway in the thirties and from this moment the tradition started of passing that robe along to the most experienced chorus girl, or boy, at each opening."

Previous holders are there, including Casey, and all our cast wanders onstage as the current holder, a girl from *Dirty Rotten Scoundrels,* enters wearing this gypsy robe, which is traditionally decorated by each cast. Someone else is wearing the previous robe, which has been on display in the Smithsonian, and very impressive it is, too, with one arm being a complete puppet from *Avenue Q.* So the winner is read out and it is Emily Hsu; and we all form into a circle on the stage and she walks around three times counterclockwise, while we touch her and her robe for good luck. This is all videoed and indeed is very jolly and wonderful and I am so glad I came. Soon everyone wishes us good luck and then leaves us to it.

Casey says, "All right, everybody, just one chorus of 'Knights of the Round Table'"; and right there onstage the whole company take up their positions and do the song and dance routine. This is so sensible and so centering and such a smart thing to do that I admire Casey and his brilliance all over again. We are bonded and we are centered and we are ready. Nothing much for an author to do except hang around and wait for the PR folks to deliver me up to the press.

At five to six I am taken out and grilled in front of the Shubert Theatre for the world press, then I'm led along Shubert Alley into the Booth Theatre next door, where the Pythons are being held downstairs. I kiss Terry and Terry and Mike and John, who are all looking distinguished, and there is John's wife, Alyce Faye, already in tears in her kindly way, overjoyed by the whole emotion of the experience. She is particularly perceptive in the things she says. Michael Palin is also very generous about my *Greedy Bastard Diary* and seems surprised at the intimacy of it all. This from the diary writer supreme.

All the Pythons seem to be at ease and looking forward to seeing it, sipping drinks in the mirrored bar downstairs. We are all anxious to get on with it and soon the relatives are shepherded away and we are left waiting on the stairs. It all feels strangely familiar. Even to Graham sadly not being there. John physically pushes Mike around like a schoolboy.

"You still can't keep your hands off him, can you," I say and we are once again that odd group of strange men backstage waiting to go on.

We are led out to face the electrical storm of the cameras. There is cheering and screaming from the crowd across the street. Within seconds our image is appearing on Australian news websites. We are all gracious and affectionate and it takes only a few moments and we disgorge into the celebrity-packed theater. Whoopi Goldberg says hello. I spy

Barbara Walters and Mike Wallace, and Lorne Michaels is there and nods and there is a general air of anticipation.

Soon the lights dim, and the overture plays to laughter and we are off with "Finland."

At the intermission I hurry down to the backstage, passing via the bar, grabbing a free cocoa from the house managers. The audience comes thudding downstairs behind me, only to discover that by order of the producers the bars are not open. We all laugh at that. Mike is outraged.

"What else did they have to decide?" he asks scornfully. "That and having the press in the other night." He is still bitter about too many press in on Tuesday, which dampened the response in the orchestra section.

As I emerge for act 2, somebody grabs me and goes on about their husband and how dare he and what a bastard and not a word about the play and I'm thinking *Honey, this is my opening night!* How much do I have to put up with? This is the very last thing I want to hear at this moment. How much of a saint must I be? Luckily I am rescued by Tania, who senses I'm cornered. As we sit down she says Michael Palin is in tears, he is so moved by it all. Terry Jones has an upset stomach and has done a runner, and I don't spot Terry Gilliam and soon it's curtain up for act 2. I watch John Cleese, laughing away farther down the aisle, and of course the Jew number lands like a hand grenade and we are golden. . . .

I thought the show went really well, especially for an

opening night. Mike hated the audience, and the cast also thought they were down; but the audience experienced the most joyous and loudest-laughing opening night in a long time. At the end the cheers were deafening and when Tim Curry kindly called up the author, I got a huge ovation. After me came Mike and then Casey and then John Du Prez, and we all took a bow. Urged to speak I said, "I really must ask up a group from Britain without whom we wouldn't all be here today: John . . . er, Paul, George, and Ringo," which got a good laugh and then I pulled up the Pythons, who apparently all made obeisance behind me, which I never saw because I was looking at my daughter's face in the front row and smiling at her, and feeling such relief that she had made it.

Standing there onstage feeling the warmth and enormous love from the audience for the uniqueness of all the Pythons being up there was a memorable moment. Mike P. was in tears. John, too, had a tear in his eye and kissed me and said well done. It was all fantastic, really. And then we cued the music and we all sang "Always Look on the Bright Side" again and the curtain came down and there was a great deal of hugging.

The Ratfuck* was held at Roseland, and was big and loud and meaty. Roast beef and Yorkshire pud were served in

---

* Mike Nichols coined the term *Ratfuck* for any large organized black-tie event.

front of a huge castle built out of Spam cans, a huge cartoon Holy Grail in the center of it. I was interviewed and photographed once again. These events now have no center. They are all surface. It is all about the hype. The Python photo is already flashing round the world. But the first night is actually the thirty-second night and the press has already been. There is still a red carpet and I do my bit talking to the journalists. I almost escape but I am caught near the door by a series of well-wishers. Nice people crowd around me. They all look impressed. They all have something great to say. Buck and Irene Henry are glowing with enthusiasm. Tom Hoberman is in tears. A lawyer crying! Elliot Brown, my Broadway lawyer, asks *do I know how rare this is?* In twenty years of going to the theater only three times can he remember an opening like this. Our old attorney Ina Meibach is there. Edie Falco (again) said she couldn't wait to bring her friends. Roger Waters loved it. I'm glad he was there. Pink Floyd was one of the original investors in the Holy Grail movie. They will continue to make money from this. Coco Schwab comes to get me and drag me over to a grinning David Bowie, who is standing with Lou Reed and the adorable Iman. They all say nice things. In particular, they both think Sara is a gold mine and they have the idea to make money from her. I tell them—Too late!

After about an hour I try and grab some food, but there is no seafood or veggie or dessert, it is a true Ratfuck. Tania tries to pull me away to dance, but there is no escaping the crush of people who all want to come up and say well done. Steve Martin with Anne and of course Lorne; April Gornik and Eric Fischl, the great artists. Hugs from Sandra, Michael Kamen's widow, and his brother, Johnny Kamen. We weep a little at the loss of Michael and how much he would have loved this. Basil Pao, the photographer and graphic artist of The Rutles album, is grinning and introduces me to his daughter, who is sixteen. I think his wife Pat was pregnant when I last saw her, on a visit to Cheung Chau Island off Hong Kong.

My old accountant and friend Ian Miles finds me and is animated and wants to meet Jane Tani, our business manager, and talk. I hope he finds her. The place is a zoo. I finally manage to dance with my wife, only she insists I must dance with Sara. Now this is a first for Tania. Never in my entire life has she delivered me voluntarily into the hands of another woman. Certainly not on the dance floor, which is where I met and fell in love with her. Fortunately, Sara is not really interested in dancing but wants me to meet her father and mother, who are divorced and all staying with her. She has already told me how tiny her apartment is. When I finally manage to return to my wife for a dance, Tamar insists on circling us and photographing us, until I ask her to please go away.

Is there no *real* anywhere anymore?

FRIDAY, MARCH 18, 2005

Next morning I walked into Sardi's, where all the producers were having lunch, and they stood up and applauded. The box office was going nuts. The reviews apparently are sensational, though I stuck to my guns and didn't read them. We had done by then more than $900,000 at the box office that morning. By 2 p.m. we passed the million-dollar mark in a single day, and by the evening performance we were already over two million and making Broadway history. So, not just a great show, not just great reviews, but great box office, too.

That night, I returned to watch the opening of the show. The audience is electric. The house is huge and hot. The cast on a high. They have their massive audience response back, and they are a bona fide hit now. My old pal Carey Harrison, the novelist and playwright, is in from Cambridge with his kids. It's a joy to see him. I told everybody that for me the Pythons being there made the evening; and it's true, they did.

Steve Martin said presciently, "They will never forgive you for this."

We dine with the family after the show. At Orso's, Joel Siegel gives me a wave and tells me what he said on the show. "Tony Soprano" (well, James Gandolfini) smiles and nods and says congratulations. Terry Gilliam's whole table of family applauds and gives me a thumbs-up. They have all loved the show. Terry comes over and gives me twenty minutes of generous personal enthusiasm on how great it all is. He seems very excited. Everyone involved with this show is beaming these days.

SATURDAY, MARCH 19, 2005

Emotional farewells onstage from all the cast. I told them before that I am leaving, and now they all come and hug me. Some of the girls have a little tear. Jenny Hill weeping. Sara is choked up. Even cheery Abbey is glum. How adorable they all are. How much I shall miss them. John Cleese said on opening night that he envies them getting to do this show together every night. And I do, too, but most of all I will miss seeing them onstage.

Salman Rushdie comes to the show and afterwards we sup at Angus McIndoe's. The restaurant is loud and wearing. I am beginning to weaken now. Had enough. Time to go home and be normal. It's hard to pretend an emotion everyone is foisting on you. There are emails from around the world. It's not that I'm unhappy, it's just that this is not the stuff of happiness. Success is a short-lived illusion. It's hard to last longer than the next day. We have known the show was funny for some months now, but it's nice to have the vindication of the critics. I keep telling everyone that for me the real greatness was being onstage with the Pythons again. It's true. That was an historic moment.

LEAVING NEW YORK

SUNDAY, MARCH 20, 2005

In a foul temper all day as my family pack and go. All my boarding school anxiety is back. Finally I manage to slip into a calmer, exhausted state and apologize to both wife and child for my grumpiness. The pressure has finally got to me. *I want to be home.* Everyone says you must be so happy, but as Tania says, it hasn't sunk in yet. I am being kept on for Charlie Rose and Elvis Mitchell tomorrow, then I can fly.

HOMEWARD BOUND

MONDAY, MARCH 21, 2005

So I'm outta here. Sitting at the Newark airport two hours early, shoes scanned, underpants clear of dangerous devices, flirting madly with the Continental gatekeepers to let me into the OnePass lounge. It actually took me a couple of passes, but it worked. Both ladies perked up well to an elderly Python, although I politely denied being in *A Fish Called Wanda*. Even the security guys seemed *Spamalot* conscious, allowing me through the scanner without removing my shoes.

First thing this morning I had a fantastic interview with Charlie Rose upstairs at Sardi's, where he grilled me about everything. We both had a great time. Then I rolled over to the Museum of Television for an interview with Elvis Mitchell. Unfortunately, Elvis had left the building. Indeed, he had left the town. He was in LA. Not only that but he'd got the time screwed up, so he wasn't even there to interview me online. So there we are.

I hopped into MoMA and had a quick eye blitz of my favorite floor, the fifth, stuffed with fabulous Magrittes, Picassos; one nude in particular with hands crossed reminded me of a Roman matron from Pompeii, the same tones and hairstyle. Coupla great Van Goghs, the magnificent olive trees and the night sky side by side. A lovely Hopper of a gas station at night, though not as big as Steve Martin's Hopper of a magnificent lady waiting patiently in a hotel lobby. His art last night was utterly ridiculous, a Bacon and a Freud sitting together with a Picasso and his Fischls.

Elvis Mitchell called to apologize abjectly. He is never late, he said. And here's the great joke: his ex-girlfriend is Tiara, my late PR woman who was always late.

"Is this some kind of great cosmic joke?" I asked him.

He wants to apologize some more but I cut him short. "I'm not in the least upset," I said. "I had a great time, plus I didn't have to sit and talk about myself."

So now it's all over and I'm homeward bound, and for God's sake we pulled it off. There is a rave from John Lahr in *The New Yorker* waiting for me to read, which Charlie Rose kept quoting, and, yes, I will read that because I know John

Lahr and, dammit, he is practically family, being married to Connie Booth and all.

Did I learn anything? Probably yes. First, Mike's law: Only work with the best. Second, Mike's second law: Never settle for anything less than the best. Third: Never give up. Fourth: Always work with Mike. That's about it for showbiz laws, I think.

When Mike became involved, the whole thing became a class act. He led gently and persuasively from the front with the obsessional quality required to never let go or put up with the second-rate. He is a tireless man, with a minimal capacity for sleep, and possessing a brilliant backup partner in the wonderful Diane Sawyer. Significantly, after her visits to Chicago major changes were always effected. Now that's a partnership. The fact that she adores him and thinks he might leave her at any stage for hundreds of other women who surround him—as she said to me at lunch—is a very dear measure of her and her love for him. As if he would.

Tim Curry told me he loved watching people alone in the dark with tears in their eyes when he was singing "I'm All Alone," and how Diane came into his dressing room and burst into tears at the thought of that song. Mike's insistence on a star cast was fine and right and exactly not what I wanted. But he was right, right, right; and now even though the show is the star, it is packed with wondrous actors: David Hyde Pierce, who volunteered; Hank Azaria, who Mike picked; and Tim Curry, who was always my first choice. What Mike did was to find the very best and finest. Casey was a brilliant call. His first gig, too. Sara is about to be a star, Christian Borle is a comedy genius, Hank is a pillar of laughs, and Christopher Sieber, who came in at just the right time, is extraordinary. Mike is probably the best casting director in the business.

Mike's other great call was to call in the English. It is panto after all, but the sheer class of Tim Hatley, with his amazing sets and freakishly great costumes, and the sparkling lighting of Hugh Vanstone have made the whole production glow like a gem. People are happy the moment they walk into the theater, from the moment they see the portcullis and the towers and the Gilliam clouds, they feel comfortable and secure. Once the stage is filled with the vibrant colors of Finland, they know they are in firm hands. Was ever such a brief gag so brilliantly caparisoned? We make a joke of the very *fact* of an opening number, so by the time we get to "I'm Not Dead Yet" and the whole cart of bodies explodes into dance—dead bodies that we were sure were just dummies—it takes the audience so by surprise that they gurgle with delight and they are ours. They scream with joy at the Laker Girls and the whole silliness of it, and are then knocked sideways by "The Song That Goes Like This," even applauding the Andrew Lloyd Webber chandelier descending. From then on, act 1 plays swiftly through, thanks to Mike's smartness in cutting the witch burning and the "Cow Song." "Find Your Grail" works first as a send-up of such a song, and then surprisingly as a real song that goes like that, so that there is a spine-tingling emotional reaction when Sara emerges and countersings her gospel song. Then we do not milk the applause, which could be there for at least three minutes, but move straight on, garnering the goodwill and keeping the benefit for later. Oh yes, it is a smart little show and no mistake.

Mike was even right about the end of the first act and his obsession with "Run Away." He said that they could not be running away if the castle did not move and he kept right on about this until now the castle does indeed move away from us on animation. The animals come flying over the battlements and the first disastrous rabbit-falling effect we abandoned is replaced by a cartoon version that crushes the word *intermission*, so that the act ends theatrically and cinematically and cartoonishly at the same time. And there we are at the intermission with them wanting more.

We immediately hit them in act 2 with a familiar favorite, the Knights of Ni, and then lull them into something like a sigh of satisfaction as we segue into "Always Look on the Bright Side." Now they have something they are familiar with and fond of and they bask in the good nature of Michael McGrath's Patsy cheering up King Arthur and teaching him how to whistle and the yellow umbrella *Singing in the Rain* tap-dancing. Soon comes the Sir Robin song, which they adore, and that unexpectedly segues into the Black Knight, which works wonders, thanks to my ad-lib gag "Arms for the poor," which audiovisual pun covers the necessary shift to enable Chris Sieber to complete the move so he can become legless as well. The finest moment in the show for me follows. What Mike calls the Jew song. What John and I have more discreetly titled "You Won't Succeed on Broadway," the number Marsha Brooks thought would be cut and several Pythons could not see the point of, but which stops the entire show. This is the number that really rocks them in their seats, first the daring, outrageous statement of a simple perceptible truth, "You won't succeed on Broadway if you don't have any Jews."

Something so unexpectedly gentile and yet good-willed that they hold their breaths a tiny second in case it should go foul, but, no, it doesn't! And when David Hyde Pierce goes into his *Fiddler on the Roof* dance, they scream and shriek and cannot believe it and, yes, of course, we really *are* going to do the bottle dance with little Holy Grails on their heads and there is genuine ecstasy in the room. Saturday at the back of the mezzanine, where I was watching, some guys even got to their feet. A standing ovation in the middle of a number.

This is the high point of our show, but it is by no means the end of the unexpected. My old SNL comedy writer pal Alan Zweibel reveled in the fact he could never predict which way it was going—and who indeed could predict

Lancelot would "come out" in a full "Rio" number with boys in outrageous orange costumes, that out–Peter Allen's everything. Who could foresee the poignant ballad of Arthur's "I'm All Alone" as he completely ignores his poor companion, Patsy? Or that the Grail would be found under the front row of the orchestra and the lucky seat holder dragged up onstage to receive an Arthur and be hymned and photographed? All these ideas—which came sometimes in the solitary writing cell and sometimes in the fury of rehearsal and sometimes in the desperation of a hotel room—all have combined and become somehow more than the sum of their parts, so that frequently they feel like things that were already there. Underlying secrets just waiting to be revealed that feel so right it seems impossible they weren't always present and indeed aren't in the movie. And yet act 2 isn't the movie at all. Is it really true that Robin was never a watchman and a bringer out of dead people before enlisting as a knight? Or that Lance wasn't his pal and co-watchman who enlists alongside him, so that now we have a real story about two friends in Arthur's army, who join him to find not only the Grail but their own grails, Lance in his love for Herbert (and curtains) and Robin in his love for musical theater. And how appropriate that the whole thing ends up on Broadway, the Holy Grail of musical theater.

So now it's over and I'm home, but not for long. Unexpectedly the Tony fairy showers us with fourteen Tony nominations.

Musical: *Monty Python's Spamalot*
Book (Musical): Eric Idle
Original Musical Score: John Du Prez and Eric Idle
Actor (Musical): Hank Azaria, Tim Curry
Actor (Featured Role—Musical): Michael McGrath,
    Christopher Sieber
Actress (Featured Role—Musical): Sara Ramirez
Director (Musical): Mike Nichols
Choreographer: Casey Nicholaw
Orchestrations: Larry Hochman
Scenic Design (Musical): Tim Hatley
Costume Design (Musical): Tim Hatley
Lighting Design (Musical): Hugh Vanstone

I have never been much of a man for awards. Just as well,
you might say, but these Tony Awards are a big deal, especially the most coveted award for Best Musical. They can
make the difference between recoupment or closure. Many
shows hang around till June in the hope of an award that
will keep them open. This is explained to me by our producers and I am asked to fly to New York for a press junket.
Sure, why not. Tania is delighted to come with me and it's
great fun for us to see the show again. It's even more fun
joining the cast junketing, though I don't see much of the
cast as we are rattled around from interview to interview.
Mike and I also attend the Drama Desk Awards and the
Drama League Awards and the Theater World Awards and

some other awards I forget. It's wonderful seeing Mike even if it is at photo shoots and gala luncheons.

One night Bill Haber asks me if I will escort someone special to the show. Tania and I were already going, so I said sure, no problem. This is how I met Steve Wynn. He would make a significant difference to the success of our show.

DIVA LAS VEGAS

It's early springtime in New York, 2005, and I'm in a dark and crowded Shubert Theatre lobby, looking for a billionaire. No, I'm not looking for a date. *Spamalot* is playing to packed houses and our producer Bill Haber has asked me to escort someone very important to the show tonight.

"This is vital to our future," says Bill, and as he is unable to stay for the show tonight, he asks me if I will sit in the theater with this VIP.

"Sure," I say.

Tania and I love going to the show anyway; and in the lobby I meet and greet Steve Wynn, the billionaire owner of the Wynn hotel, Las Vegas. He is friendly and we sit beside him as the curtain rises. The play has only been on five minutes when Steve leans in, grips my knee, and whispers in my ear: "Eric," he says, "this will be great in Las Vegas."

"Yes," I say, "it will."

Then I realize disappointedly he means *Spamalot*. My future as a billionaire's date is still up for grabs. But he loves the show. He adores the show. More importantly, he wants the show. He is going to buy it for Las Vegas.

"Can I give you a ride home?" he asks nicely.

I'm thinking Sixth Avenue, but he means LA.

Well, *okay*.

Next day he flies us home in a plane bigger than my old boarding school. There are dogs on board, so my wife is happy. She plays with them. They are friendly, but one word in German and they would tear us apart. So we don't say any word in German. All the way back to LA Steve plays the *Spamalot* soundtrack, regaling his passengers with his version of scenes from the show. Later he leaves a message on my phone in a British accent so good I think for a moment it is Hank Azaria.

A month later he flies me to Las Vegas to stay at the Wynn hotel and see the car park that is to be our new home. Not only has he bought the Vegas rights for *Spamalot*, he wants to build a brand-new theater for it. He believes Broadway is the next big wave of entertainment there.

I am put into a suite that has enough room for half a dozen people. I wake early and search the many rooms, but I can find no one. There is only me. So I head out for a walk. By eight in the morning it's already stinking hot in Las Vegas. Not just hot, it's blindingly light. There is simply too much of the stuff bouncing around by the pool, bouncing off the walls at the speed of light, shuffling across the desert blown by the wind that lifts the awnings on the striped pavilions and ruffles the tassels and snaps the umbrellas. This is the only time you can be alone in Las Vegas, though there are still one or two early risers amongst the empty white ranks of the poolside loungers. While the waiters chatter over the endless piped-in disco beat, the gardeners spray water over the Provençal greenery. There is half a forest of huge pines, impressively green on their hillside, transported here into the desert and tastefully disported amongst the rocks and artificial waterfalls. Even the crickets are chirruping, though I am suspicious and notice they have also been piped in. Now and again a six-foot-large frog pops up out of the water and sings.

I decide I almost prefer the fake to the real. Hardly surprising: I am in show business, which is all about faking the real. I think I prefer it here because it's less smelly. Certainly in the case of Venice. The beauty of ancient places is accidental. Nobody planned it that way. The fake seems somehow more intended. To stand in front of the phony Doge's Palace at eleven and hear the chimes of Big Ben from London, the pealing of the church bells from Paris, and the explosion of a volcanic waterfall is to experience something unintended and unplannable. A random universe created by an infinite number of monkeys.

I am a little concerned about how *Spamalot* will play, out here in the desert. I decide to visit all the major attractions and see exactly what's on offer to the punters who spend only two and a half days here on average. There are more than seventy shows, so I start with the big ones. First, I went to see *Jubilee!*, but there were no Jews in it. The popularity of the show is evident when the curtain rises and the plot immediately grips me with its thrilling story of a hundred bare-breasted ladies seducing Samson and causing the *Titanic* to sink. Nothing quite matches the intensity of this production that brings onstage almost a hundred men in little black jockstraps and a hundred topless ladies to reenact the biblical tale of Samson and Delilah. It's not quite the story I remember from school, but a nicely built young African American simulates sex with an ancient lady masquerading as the siren seductress who brought down the man who brought down the house.

Then for some unaccountable reason the story shifted to Southampton, where the *Titanic* was about to set sail on its maiden voyage. The captain's ball revealed a young captain hopelessly in love and a drunken horny American wife in search of some stokers belowdecks. These she found and while disporting herself erotically with them, the ship struck an iceberg and water poured in and all the sailors were drowned, although she unaccountably survived on a lifeboat, waving her arms around in a paroxysm of grief, as the ship went down onstage, firing off rockets of distress. I knew how it felt.

The scene then shifted suddenly to New York, where a crowd of cheerleader girls in red, white, and blue spandex sang "I'm a Yankee Doodle Dandy." I'm still unsure what this referred to. Sometimes the plot was a little hard to follow. To me the most interesting part of the show was a scene where the girls started nude and gradually put on more clothing. An odd though effective technique, which I wish more ladies would employ.

Jubilee! has been on for years and so I decided to check out the more modern French competition. At the Crazy Horse the girls have blond wigs, perfect derrieres, and genuine French names like Fifi and Suki. They remind me what the seventies was all about: light shows and shagging. But the show is a little thin on plot. And clothing.

Currently, the Wynn itself has two shows: on the main stage the extremely funny and naughty puppet show *Avenue Q*, direct from Broadway. It is an intimate show and it seems a little lost in a huge proscenium arch theater. Also the selling line is terrible: *Come see what all the fuzz is about.* The show itself is actually very good and very funny.

Next door is *Le Rêve*, a water show in the round, named after his own Picasso painting that Steve Wynn accidentally put his elbow through. The circular theater is lovely, although this new show is fighting a battle against its own technology, which on the night I attend it sadly loses. The show is shut down and we all have to leave.

The rest of the entertainment is mainly French-Canadian, from Celine Dion to the many cirques. Tim Hatley and I went together to the Celine Dion show, which was exactly like a Celine Dion show. Tim rolled his eyes.

"Not exactly panto," we agreed.

The best of Vegas are the many Cirque du Soleil shows, of which *O* is the most genius.

Monty Python was a *flying* circus, but does that qualify us as a cirque? We have no acrobats, no contortionism apart from Silly Walks, and only a few French people yelling abuse while farting in our general direction. What will the nipple-sated Nevadans make of our little show? One thing for sure, you cannot out-Vegas Vegas. There is simply no parodying this. There is no over the top. Only over the topless.

I know upfront that I will have to cut twenty minutes from the show. What Fitzgerald said of American lives is definitely true of Vegas—there are no second acts. Partly this is because they want you back in the casino, and partly it's because they want you back in the casino, but mainly it's because they want you back in the casino. In fact, with our low ticket prices ($49, $69, $89) I figured out that you will actually *save* money if you go and spend ninety minutes at *Spamalot*. Even on the cheapest slots. And if you sleep during the show, you can save on a room.

Surely to cut twenty minutes won't be that difficult? The original movie was only eighty-three, so how hard can it be?

Will it be harder in Nevada?

(A slogan I am trying to sell the tourist board.)

Steve Wynn has bought not only the rights for Las Vegas, but also all the West Coast touring rights. He wants citizens of San Francisco, LA, and San Diego to come and see *Spamalot* in Vegas. Incredibly, we suddenly have a path to profit.

But fate has one more final surprise for us at the Tony Awards.

SUNDAY, JUNE 5, 2005

I'm in New York at Radio City Music Hall for the 2005 Tony Awards. The *Spamalot* producers are here, the nervous nominees are here, and we're all crammed into penguin suits for what is billed as Broadway's most glamorous night, though I always thought that was Sir Ian McKellen. We've been groomed and buffed and cosseted and polished; and Tania is looking very glamorous in some magnificent jewelry—a necklace, earrings, and a rather lovely expensive purple ring—which we have been loaned for the duration of the show by Harry Winston, the Fifth Avenue jeweler, who first began the trend of lending sparklers to the stars at awards shows like this. We have had a lot of fun choosing thousands of dollars of diamonds to bedeck the lovely neck of Tania and the final thing she chose was this beautiful purple amethyst ring, which she loves. During the reception that precedes the affair, Pinkerton operatives hover close, keeping a sharp eye on the millions of dollars of designer jewelry that sparkles on the ears and throats of many a glamorous Broadway star anxiously awaiting tonight's results.

"Just keeping an eye out for you," says one burly quarter-back of a security guy who sees me looking at him. The only drawback is that, Cinderella like, we must return the bau-bles to the store immediately once the night is over.

I have to admit that I have never seen a Tony show be-fore. It seems when God was doling out the showbiz DNA, I missed out on the Tony gene, although I do love musical theater, having grown up in a world of Gilbert and Sullivan before switching into a mature respect for Frank Loesser, Richard Rodgers, Oscar Hammerstein, Cole Porter, and Lerner and Loewe. So, yes, I am rather fond of musical com-edy, though I have found the comedy bit has been noticeably absent for the last twenty years. It's all been a little too MTV with helicopters landing onstage, and underground boats in Parisian sewers peopled with people with plates on their faces. Not a laugh in sight. So we must thank the great and glorious Mel Brooks for mercifully reviving the virtually extinct musical comedy form, opening *The Producers* at the St. James Theatre on April 19, 2001. I was there that night and, as the audience howled in joy, I thought to myself, *Now they will take* Spamalot *seriously. . . .*

And they did.

Tonight, most of the audience of all sexes is drooling over Hugh Jackman, who is hosting the awards. Tania and I are seated about halfway back in the hall, and about halfway through the show I see Mike Nichols urgently heading up the aisle towards me. By then of the fourteen Tonys we have been nominated for we have already lost six. Not a single win. Mike reaches me.

"They're going to stiff us," he says. "You have to think of something to say."

In a previous wifetime I used to write ad-libs for David Frost, so I am not unqualified for this task.

"I'll have a go."

Mike returns glumly to his seat, and I start racking my brains for something amusing to say that won't sound bitter and twisted but, on the contrary, incredibly mature and suitably grateful for being ignored and passed over completely. It's a bit like trying to write an altar speech for a jilted bride and I am so far into my task of trying to think of something funny and grown-uppy to say, which has barely progressed beyond "Yah boo sucks, and we don't really mind because we do this stuff for laughs, not for statuettes, and Monty Python never got any awards—no Oscars, no Grammys, no Emmys, no Tonys, no Ritas, no Peters, no Ivors, no Conchitas—and that didn't hurt us any," that I barely notice when I personally lose the next award for best book of a musical.

Advised by the virtually irresistible Hugh Jackman that this would be a good time, my gorgeous wife in her glittering jewelry exits to the bathroom under the watchful eye of a burly Pinkerton, during what is promised as a long commercial break. She has barely left her seat when she is instantly replaced by a mature lady with a large and very bizarre hat that resembles nothing so much as a ginger tomcat squatting on her head. It is axiomatic that there must be no empty seats visible at TV awards shows. Consequently highly dressed extras are employed to deftly slide into the gaps the minute someone heads for the bathroom or pops out for a nervous nicotine break. Of course, this is the very moment the cameras single out me and "my wife" for our close-up as we bravely lose for best original musical score.

I am so busy trying not to laugh at this woman, smiling proudly by my side, giggling in the knowledge that people all over America are going, "Whatever happened to Tania?" and "Has he gone mad, taking up with an elderly cat woman?" that I don't even have time to feel any disappointment. We have, after all, been to several Broadway award ceremonies recently and Mike has picked up a variety of oddly shaped statuettes and made a series of increasingly funny speeches. My favorite, when yet again his name was announced, was watching him walk up slowly, look genuinely puzzled at the audience, and say sadly, "I miss failure."

Well, tonight the pigeons of irony are certainly coming home to roost as we continue to miss out on best choreography, best sets, best costumes, best new shoes, etc., etc. Finally the Tony fairy relents and the utterly deserving Sara Ramirez heads up the aisle to pick up the Tony for Best Actress in a Featured Role in a Musical and to thank us, her parents, and Claritin. And then, of course, Mike's nightmare is over as he inevitably wins yet another Tony for best director of a musical. I crumple up my pathetic half-written one-liners in relief.

But fate has one more surprise in store for us. After a very long and occasionally interesting evening, the inestimable Hugh Jackman reads out the winner of the best musical of 2005 and incredibly and surprisingly it's *Monty Python's Spamalot*. Wow! Who would have thunk it? Our cast of knights and wenches spill out on to Hugh Jackman, whooping and hollering and hugging, and the auditorium is filled with beaming producers hurriedly heading for the stage. I beat them to it by a good yard and a half, Mike gives me a proud hug, and I barely restrain myself from kissing Hugh Jackman. (There'll be other opportunities.)

We dance the night away, of course. And at the end of the evening, there is a strange coda. On the way home our limo stops off at the side door of Harry Winston. It's after midnight and Tania sadly pulls off the earrings, removes the glittering necklace from her glorious neck, and reluctantly slips off her finger the very expensive purple amethyst ring. I take the package inside. In an office close by, a Pinkerton sits in shirtsleeves behind a large desk, taking back all the jewelry. I hand over the goodies and sign. In case I had second thoughts, I notice prominently on the desk in front of him is a .38 Police Special. . . .

We drive home. The limo does not turn into a pumpkin.

Next morning I got up early and went to Harry Winston's, where I bought the expensive amethyst ring for Tania. She was surprised, thrilled, and overjoyed. After all, we had just won the Tony for best musical on Broadway!

So it was the Ring cycle after all.

AFTERWORD

Back on Broadway, baby!
"And so we return again! Unexpectedly!"

The Knights who say Ni!

OPENING KNIGHT, ST. JAMES THEATRE

THURSDAY, NOVEMBER 16, 2023

Incredibly, *Spamalot* is back on Broadway. And this time my tears are not just of laughter. Standing amidst a blissed-out crowd who are on their feet happily singing my song "Always Look on the Bright Side of Life," I feel tears coursing down my cheeks and I weep unashamedly for Mike, for Casey, for Bill, for those we have lost like the wonderful Michael McGrath, and the unexpected joy of the return of the show we first opened almost twenty years ago. Gazing around at the standing ovation, with Tania beside me, of course wearing her beautiful purple amethyst ring, and my daughter Lily with Charlie and a handmade Holy Grail handbag, I feel so lucky to have lived and survived to see *Spamalot* back on Broadway at the magnificent St. James Theatre. Yes, I thought they would laugh—the show has been making 'em laugh round the world for two decades—but what I had not expected was the way I would feel, tearing up so many times during the evening, nor the way Broadway greeted our return with packed houses and rave notices which, to my amazement, were even better this time round. As the gold confetti fell from the ceiling, and the audience cheered and sang along, I was moved by the thought that this show will still be bringing joy and laughter to people long after I'm gone.

That is a very powerful feeling.

ACKNOWLEDGMENTS

I would like to thank Casey Nicholaw for all his amazing input into the original show. And for spending five years with me on a fruitless struggle to turn it into a movie. He was the heart and soul of our production. Thanks, too, to Bill Haber, who bought the show, for his continued friendship and support.

A big thank-you to Jeffrey Finn, for bringing his sold-out Kennedy Center production from Washington back to Broadway and beyond. He made a lucky man very happy to see it open on Broadway twice in a lifetime. To my doctor friend David Kipper, who discovered my pancreatic cancer very early, and to my surgeon Dr. Nicholas Nissen, for promptly removing it. I owe you both my life and the chance to see the second coming on Broadway.

This production that once finished its limited run there in spring 2024 will begin a major tour of North America in the fall of 2025. So watch out for it in your local cities. If you need a laugh, or cheering up, then please don't miss it!

Thank you to my creative partner, John Du Prez, for his brilliant music, and a big thank-you to the amazing Josh Rhodes for directing and choreographing this wonderful production. Mike Nichols would be proud of you. Thanks to Steve Martin for playing God, to Tania for being God, and thanks as always to Tom Hoberman, my lawyer, and Matt Bialer, my agent, for selling this book, and Matthew Inman, my editor, for buying it. A huge thank-you, too, to Steve Spiegel and Theatrical Rights Worldwide for shepherding our work around the world, and all the actors and singers and backstage people who have made *Spamalot* a global hit. And one final big thank-you to the audience who so welcomed *Spamalot* into their hearts. May you continue to enjoy it for many years.

Say no more!

ABOUT THE AUTHOR

Eric Idle, star of stage, screen, and crossword puzzle, has often been compared to Noël Coward. But never favorably. He has been in show business since 1961. "Unfortunately, I can't find the exit," he says. "My role in life seems to be cheering people up," he adds glumly.

His song "Always Look on the Bright Side of Life," coincidentally the title of his bestselling *Sortabiography,* has been the number one most requested ditty at British funerals for more than twenty years. He performed it live before two billion people at the London 2012 Olympic Games closing ceremony and coincidentally it also appears in the Tony Award–winning Best Musical of the Year 2005 Broadway hit *Monty Python's Spamalot*, which he wrote with John Du Prez, and which returned to Broadway in

November 2023 with rave reviews and packed houses before touring North America again. His latest book, *The Spamalot Diaries,* is an intimate look at the making of that show.

Spamalot opened in Melbourne in 2007, the same year Eric and John premiered *Not the Messiah (He's a Very Naughty Boy),* a comic oratorio based on *The Life of Brian,* at the Sydney Opera House, with a full orchestra and chorus, which then toured Australia and New Zealand.

His new show, coincidentally called *Always Look on the Bright Side of Life, Live!,* is a nostalgic one-man musical reflecting his love of comedy, music, life, and what he calls mock and roll, a hybrid of comedy and music, with tributes to George Harrison and Robin Williams and a salute to *The Rutles,* the Beatles-parody movie he created, which was the world's first ever mockumentary about the legendary pre-fab four whose legend will last a lunchtime.

Eric is a rare survivor of pancreatic cancer and proudly supports PanCAN and Standup2Cancer, and this will be his first full tour of the antipodes since surviving. On his last visit to Australia, in November 2022, he performed a sold-out show at the State Theatre in Sydney with Shaun Micallef and closed the Just for Laughs Festival that year, co-incidentally, singing his theme song with all the comedians at the Sydney Opera House.

He has lived in LA since 1994 with his wife, Tania, and daughter, Lily, where they experienced the earthquake, and decided to stay. He has a son, Carey, who very smartly lives on the Sunshine Coast, from a previous wifetime to Lyn Ashley, an Australian actress. Eric has written several novels and plays and he was in several movies but he forgets which.

Oh and he was in Monty Python.

Will this do?